ASSURANCE OF SALVATION

John R. Mumaw

Cover Photo: Kevin D. Shank

Christian Light Publications, Inc.
Harrisonburg, VA 22801
1989

Copyright © 1989
Christian Light Publications, Inc.

ISBN: 0-87813-955-9
Printed in U.S.A.

Dedicated to those
who after his happy conversion
led the author to a definite
assurance of salvation

Preface to the Third Edition

Situations change, but truth is abiding. We feel the winds of shift and movement. We see the signs of change, decay, and renewal. But truth stands.

Nearly four decades ago when this book was printed in its first edition, many who are reading these pages were not yet born. Older ones remember the situation. A vacuum in teaching had left many with an unsteady assurance about their abiding relationship with God. Then this book on Biblical assurance stood up boldly in that gap and steadied many feet. In the intervening time the shaking, rumbling, and corroding work of the enemy has attacked not only assurance but the foundational doctrine of salvation itself. Whereas our fathers and mothers needed help with assurance of salvation, many of their sons and daughters are facing uncertain doctrine about salvation.

In this third edition Brother Mumaw, aged now and yet aware of current needs in relation to this great doctrine of salvation, has written an additional introductory chapter. This first chapter presents groundwork truth—the plan of salvation. God's plan it is—simple and yet immeasurably profound. Beyond the first chapter, the headings are reworded and a few minor changes are offered, but the book remains essentially what it was. Truth stands.

May the God who still saves fallen men and women from sin upon confession of faith in His Son continue to give assurance to them by the sure promises of His Word.

JOHN A. COBLENTZ

INTRODUCTION

What Christian has not said sometime in his experience, "Yes, I know Christ can save, and I want to be saved. But how can I know for sure He has saved me?" To be saved is great, but to know we are saved gives confidence and joy. Without that the Christian life may be only a tantalizing mixture of hope and fear.

With much gratefulness I remember the minister who gave to me, early in my Christian life, a tract which treated the subject of assurance. This tract took doubt out of my mind and set me free to enjoy my Christian faith. We can be assured of a certain salvation. We must help all believers to that assurance.

There are two extreme positions to be avoided. One is that which says that assurance is presumption—that we cannot know we are saved until we have passed the judgment. Many of our elders, in a mistaken humility and diffidence, held this view and approached death with fear and trembling. The other extreme has come into our thinking from a system of theology which teaches an unconditional salvation through the choice and order of a sovereign God. According to this view, one who is saved can never become unsaved. This teaching brings an unscriptural carelessness concerning the continuance of saving faith and circumspect living. It gives a false assurance.

This book sets forth the abundant teaching of the Scriptures on the subject and carefully balances promise and condition, assurance and safeguard. I have read the manuscript with real pleasure and blessing. Any Christian can read it with profit; to some it will bring a crisis in thinking, and, we trust, a new era of Christian peace and enjoyment.

This book is adapted to private reading and also to class study. We hope that many congregations will use it for classes in Christian assurance, that older Christians may be established in their faith, and younger Christians may be led into a faith which has assurance without presumption.

PAUL ERB

CONTENTS

Preface v
Introduction vii
1. *God's Word Teaches Salvation* 1
   Salvation Is God's Plan 1
   The Provision for Salvation Is Universal 6
   Salvation Necessitates Human Response 8
   Salvation Is a Continuing Experience 11
   Salvation Is Sustained by Christian Action 14
   Salvation Is a Way of Life 18
2. *Assurance Involves a Doctrine of Experience* 22
   Assurance Pertains to Certainty of Salvation 22
   Assurance Copes With Doubt 25
   Assurance Rests on Divine Approval 27
   Assurance Is Based on Scripture 30
   Assurance Appears in Many Forms 32
3. *Some People Do Not Have Assurance* 35
   Inadequate Experience with God Leads to Uncertainty . 35
   Inadequate Knowledge of God Leads to Mistrust 36
   Inadequate Faith in God Fails to Achieve Justification . 38
   Inadequate Commitment to God Stunts Spiritual Growth 39
   Inadequate Reliance Upon God Creates Spiritual Conflicts 40
4. *Learn How to Get Assurance* 42
   Exercise Belief in the Son of God 42
   Trust the Promises of God 43
   Appropriate the Truth of God 44
   Study the Word of God 45
   Pray for the Wisdom of God 46
   Cultivate Christian Graces 46
5. *Assurance Relies on Essential Christian Experience* 49
   Forgiveness From God Is Assured to Believers 49
   Acceptance by God Is a Present Reality 51
   Adoption by God Confirms Filial Relationship 52
   The Position in Christ Qualifies for Divine Blessings ... 53
   The Possessions in Christ Are Gifts of Divine Grace ... 54
   The Privileges in Christ Come Through Divine Mediation 55
6. *Assurance Involves Essential Biblical Knowledge* 58
   The Right to Our Inheritance Is Certain 58
   The Earnest of Our Inheritance Is Given 59

    The Hope of Our Inheritance Is In Effect 62
7. *There Are Tests to Confirm Assurance* 66
    The Test of Character Involves Moral Purity 67
    The Test of Confession Involves Spiritual Cleansing 68
    The Test of Obedience Involves Divine Truth 69
    The Test of Love Involves Social Compassion 71
    The Test of Loyalty Involves God's Will 72
8. *There Are More Tests to Confirm Assurance* 77
    The Test of Perseverance Involves Consistent Practice . 77
    The Test of Conduct Involves Doing Righteousness 79
    The Test of Conscience Involves Approved Behavior ... 82
    The Test of Experience Involves Spirit Witness 84
    The Test of Belief Involves Faith in Christ 86
9. *We Heed Warnings to the Christian* 89
    Avail Yourself of Divine Grace 90
    Commit Yourself to Divine Truth 90
    Protect Yourself With Divine Righteousness 91
    Identify Yourself With Divine Revelation 92
    Subject Yourself to Divine Discipline 93
    Condition Yourself to Divine Purposes 93
10. *God Makes Provision for Victory* 96
    He Keeps Us From Falling 96
    He Keeps Deposits Available 97
    He Guards His Own 98
    He Saves Completely 99
    His Love Is Inviolable 100
    He Approved the Son 100
    He Qualified Our Advocate 101
11. *The Believer Is Responsibile for Action* 104
    Keep in Memory the Gospel 104
    Continue in the Faith 105
    Abide in Christ 106
    Continue in the Word 107
    Mortify the Deeds of the Body 108
    Hold the Beginning of Your Confidence 109
    Bibliography 111

1.

God's Word Teaches Salvation

Salvation Is God's Plan

The kingdom of God is not meat and drink, but righteousness, peace, and joy in the Holy Ghost—Romans 14:17.

The kingdom of God is the divine rule in the hearts of Christian believers. It is administered by Jesus Christ. It is operated through the ministry of the Holy Ghost. It offers salvation, the saving of people, of believing persons, from the consequences of sin.

Among the many benefits of salvation there are three distinctive elements that characterize life in the kingdom: righteousness and peace and joy in the Holy Ghost. Righteousness pertains to the will to do right. It is a moral part of God's likeness bestowed upon us which issues in right conduct and creates an awareness of acceptance with God.

Peace represents a satisfactory relationship with Jesus Christ. It also refers to personal harmony among fellow believers, which is a participation in the union and communion with the saints.

The joy in the Holy Ghost is an emotional delight derived from a sense of being in divine favor. These three elements of spiritual experience are a deepening satisfaction in our relationship with God.

1. Salvation Is Human Redemption

We have redemption through his [Christ's] blood, the forgiveness of sins according to the riches of his grace. There is therefore now no condemnation to them which are in Christ Jesus, who walk not after the flesh, but after the Spirit. For the law of the Spirit of life in Christ Jesus hath made me free from the law of sin and death—Ephesians 1:7; Romans 8:1,2.

Redemption is the process by which Christ the Redeemer purchased the deliverance of people from under the weight of sin. He offered Himself a ransom for release of sinners from condemnation. We have redemption through His blood involving the forgiveness of sins. The position of no longer being under condemnation comes by exercising faith in the atoning work of Christ.

We are not redeemed by material values but by the precious blood of Christ (I Peter 1:18). It is a deliverance from the evil desires of the flesh to a new life in the Spirit. To walk after the Spirit is to have Him regulate our thoughts and feelings. He influences the believer's conduct and directs his aspirations. The removal of condemnation opens the way for having confidence in prayer. It creates an awareness of spiritual assets in having the Holy Spirit's presence. He sets the sincere believer free from the law of sin and death.

2. Salvation Is a Spiritual Regeneration

Not by works of righteousness which we have done but according to his mercy he saved us, by washing of regeneration, and renewing of the Holy Ghost. If any man be in Christ he is a new creature: old things are passed away; behold, all things are become new—Titus 3:5; II Corinthians 5:17.

Regeneration implies a radical change affecting the whole being. It overcomes the fallen nature and focuses on the new life found in Christ. It is God's intention that all people should be partakers of this new life.

Conversion consists of repentance for sins and faith in Christ as our Saviour. Repentance and faith combined form the human response to God's offer of salvation. This experience is made real by God's action in mercy. The Holy Spirit enters the convert to bring about a change of the will, the mind, and the affections.

Jesus used the occasion of His conversation with the inquiring Nicodemus to express this great truth about salvation, saying, "Ye must be born again." Without that experience a person cannot enter the kingdom of God. By that we mean a birth into eternal life—the spiritual quality that obtains in present experience and points to our anticipated life in heaven.

3. Salvation Is a Moral Reformation

That ye put off concerning the former conversation, the old man which is corrupt according to the deceitful lusts. . . . that ye put on the new man which after God is created in righteousness and true holiness—Ephesians 4:22,24.

The moral reformation that takes place with regeneration is another aspect of salvation. It is acknowledged, however, that conversion does not at once and in a moment change the total moral behavior. The process of sanctification begins with new motivations which put into effect Christian ethical standards. These are applied to personal habits which no longer are patterned after the desires of the flesh; thus the "old man" is put off by the power of the indwelling Spirit.

Christ learned obedience through suffering. He became the author of salvation unto all them that obey Him (Hebrews 5:9). The moral disciplines that accompany regeneration involve renunciation of carnality with the cultivation of spirituality. Faith finds its expression in righteous behavior (the right way) and true (Biblical) holiness. It engages the conscience to monitor ethical choices with self-control and Christian integrity.

4. Salvation Is a Family Adoption

We are the children of God. . . . When the fulness of the time was come, God sent forth his Son . . . to redeem them that were under the law, that we might receive the adoption of sons—Romans 8:16; Galatians 4:4, 5.

It is God's intention to restore His earthly handiwork to its original purpose. This is particularly true of mankind. In the New Testament it is clear that redemption as a new birth brings believers into the family of God. We receive that adoption on the basis of God's mercy and love. We "are all the children of God by faith in Christ Jesus" (Galatians 3:26). "As many as received him, to them he gave power to become the sons of God, even to them that believe on his name" (John 1:12). "Behold, what manner of love the Father hath bestowed upon us, that we should be called the sons of God" (I John 3:1a). The children of God are blessed with the presence of Christ and with the guidance of the Holy Spirit. "As many as are led by the Spirit of God, they are the sons of God." We "have received the Spirit of adoption, whereby we cry, Abba, Father" (Romans 8:14, 15).

5. Salvation Is a Social Transformation

The wisdom that is from above is first pure, then peaceable, gentle, and easy to be intreated, full of mercy and good fruits, without partiality, and without hypocrisy—James 3:17.

The wisdom that comes from God pertains to the divine understandings He gives to those who fully trust Him. The saving effect of faith upon the heart has a direct influence upon the way we relate to other people. By the grace of God we overcome worldly patterns of living while possessing positive attitudes toward others.

With heavenly wisdom one is able to act peaceably, to be considerate of neighbors, and to exercise compassion toward people in need. Other features of this wisdom include being gentle as a servant of God, ready to forgive, and plenteous in mercy. Such a person is steady, sincere, and stable in social relationships. His inner character develops a genuine sensitivity to evil influences and cultivates peaceable relationships within the entire Christian community. His views, feelings, and conduct are consistent with God's standards in the variety of social contacts.

6. Salvation Is a Spiritual Integration

We, being many, are one body in Christ, and every one members one of another. . . . Be kindly affectioned one to another with brotherly love; in honour preferring one another—Romans 12:5, 10.

There is a vital bond in which salvation unites the life of believers with the living Christ. This same relationship establishes a community of people who have a common life together in Christ. As members of the body of Christ, we have joint commitments to the Scriptures. We accept the same doctrinal beliefs as expressed in a confession of faith. Such brotherhood faith is also expressed in common daily practices.

Because salvation brings a variety of people into the body of Christ, it brings a variety of gifts all of which call for mutual respect. All of these relationships are conditioned by a single loyalty to Christ, the Head of the body. Where the love of Christ is expressed within the brotherhood, believers honor one another within an intimate fellowship. This integration of people into a single structure of relationships as developed by the saving grace of God constitutes the Christian church.

7. Salvation Is a Divine Acceptance

Therefore being justified by faith, we have peace with God through our Lord Jesus Christ: By whom also we have access by faith into this grace wherein we stand, and rejoice in hope of the glory of God—Romans 5:1, 2.

Justification is a judicial action of forgiveness by a divine process. It is a release from guilt of moral and spiritual transgressions. That means the person has been given a favorable standing with God. Such a person is declared righteous, and his past sins are no longer held against him. Faith is credited to him as righteousness. "To him that . . . believeth on him [God] that justifieth the ungodly, his faith is counted for righteousness" (Romans 4:5).

This change in man's relationship to God assures the believer of acceptance into the kingdom of God. It represents a forgiveness that affirms release from a guilty conscience. The justified one is then able to exercise freedom with the full rights of Christian citizenship. He thereby is accepted into discipleship of the Lord Jesus Christ through whom we have acceptance with God.

8. Salvation Is a Deliverance From Wrath

Being now justified by his [Christ's] blood, we shall be saved from wrath through him. . . . For God hath not appointed us to wrath, but to obtain salvation by our Lord Jesus Christ, who died for us, that whether we wake or sleep, we should live together with him—Romans 5:9; I Thessalonians 5:9, 10.

Through redemption by the blood of Jesus, believers are excluded from a judgment against the unbelieving world. The role of redemption, as outlined in the Scriptures, has both positive and negative aspects in the process of salvation. Believers are redeemed to serve in the will of God and at the same time are set free from the judgments against evil. This is accomplished by no human merit but by the grace of God. That removes fear of God's wrath and forms the basis of spiritual triumph over evil. God's mercy and love are the basis of our salvation experience. Whether we are wide awake in the turmoil of living in a hostile society or enjoy the comforts of a peaceful community, we are granted the benefits of divine grace. Salvation is designed to provide privileges of fellowship with the people of God without any fear of wrath.

9. Salvation Is a Living Hope

Let us, who are of the day, be sober, putting on the breastplate of faith and love, and for an helmet, the hope of salvation. . . . Now the God of hope fill you with all joy and peace in believing, that ye may abound in hope, through the power of the Holy Ghost—I Thessalonians 5:8; Romans 15:13.

To be of the day is to be living in the light of the Gospel. Such living manifests the presence of faith and love. Faith believes, and in believing is filled with joy and peace. Love creates peaceful relationships. The hope of salvation comes by the indwelling of the Holy Spirit. We rely upon the God of hope to perform His purposes of redemption in due time. While waiting for the final adoption, the redemption of our bodies, we are saved by hope. Our present experience with Christ is the forerunner of eternal blessedness. Our hope adds strength and courage to remain steadfast in the commitment we have made to the will of God. We look forward in anticipation of eternal glory, which we believe will be realized at the second coming of Christ.

The Provision for Salvation Is Universal

The Son of man is come to save that which was lost. The Father sent the Son to be the Savior of the world—Matthew 18:11; I John 4:14.

The message of salvation is addressed to the lost in all parts of the world. When the aged Simeon, a just and devout saint, picked up the Baby Jesus in the temple, he "blessed God" with words of deep emotion. In his old age he reflected on the divine providence that brought "consolation" to Israel. His prayer on that occasion expressed a beautiful and significant sentiment. He addressed God saying, "Mine eyes have seen thy salvation, which thou has prepared before the face of all people" (Luke 2:30,31).

1. Salvation Rests Firmly on the Grace of God

The Lord is not slack concerning his promise, as some men count slackness; but is longsuffering to us-ward, not willing that any should perish, but that all should come to repentance—II Peter 3:9.

There is much to anticipate in the Father's house. Jesus has gone on to prepare the place for multitudes of people. The marvelous grace of God has made the message of the Gospel active in conditioning hearts of unsaved people to find salvation. He is not willing that any should be lost. His holy desire is to have all people come to the point of repentance. This divine concern is basic to our understanding of getting right with God. His grace is focused on His having taken the initiative in saving the lost. The provisions for redemption are for all who come to Him by faith in Jesus Christ. "He became the author of eternal salvation unto all them that obey him" (Hebrews 5:9).

2. Salvation Is Provided Through Jesus Christ

God commendeth his love toward us, in that, while we were yet sinners, Christ died for us. Much more then, being now justified by his blood, we shall be saved from wrath through him. For if, when we were enemies, we were reconciled to God by the death of his Son, much more, being reconciled, we shall be saved by his life—Romans 5:8-10.

Knowing that a man is not justified by the works of the law, but by the faith of Jesus Christ, even we have believed in Jesus Christ, that we might be justified by the faith of Christ, and not by the works of the law; for by the works of the law shall no flesh be justified—Galatians 2:16.

Although mention has been made of the doctrine of justification in a previous discussion, this passage points to the unfolding of a procedure to get right with God. It applies to both Gentiles and Jews. This Scripture indicates again that a sinner cannot qualify for admission into the kingdom of God by exercising self-assertions and other forms of human effort. Even the "works of the law" are ineffective to meet the universal human need for forgiveness.

The faith of Jesus Christ refers to putting our whole trust and confidence in Him to save us. Confession of faith is coupled with personal commitment to the will of God. This plan of redemption is open to all who want to be saved. It is a universal invitation to repent and believe the Gospel.

3. Salvation Is Affirmed by Jesus' Resurrection

We are buried with him by baptism into death: that like as Christ was raised up from the dead by the glory of the Father, even so we also should walk in newness of life. For if we have been planted together in the likeness of his death, we shall be also in the likeness of his resurrection—Romans 6:4,5.

Being united with Christ in a spiritual death experience is a significant aspect in the process of being saved. There is also an essential element in being identified with Christ in His resurrection. Being buried with Him and being resurrected with Him are realized "through the faith of the operation of God, who hath raised him from the dead. And you . . . hath he quickened together with him, having forgiven you all trespasses" (Colossians 2:12, 13). This introduces the effect of such a supernatural experience. It establishes the pattern of Christian behavior. To walk in "newness of life" is to live by new principles with enlarged spiritual insights and motivation. It is an adventure in love, peace, and freedom. Having put off the "old man," we "put on" the new man, "which after God is created in righteousness and true holiness" (Ephesians 4:24).

4. Salvation Is in Effect by Christ's Intercession

Christ is not entered into the holy places made with hands, which are the figures of the true; but into heaven itself, now to appear in the presence of God for us—Hebrews 9:24.

Christ's ascension consummated the earthly phase of His redemptive work. His death on the cross and His resurrection made adequate provision for the remission of sins. Then His entrance into the heavenly sanctuary established the heavenly phase of His redemptive work. Jesus' blood being fully acceptable with the Father, gained for Him a permanent priesthood, establishing an ongoing representation for Christian believers. This perpetual ministry on behalf of the redeemed by the One whose blood was fully acceptable represents His continuing work of redemption. His mediation maintains for believers a favorable standing before God. He is there interceding for all who have faith in God's plan of redemption.

5. Salvation Will Be Completed at Christ's Return

Christ was once offered to bear the sins of many; and unto them that look for him shall he appear the second time without sin unto salvation—Hebrews 9:28.

The purpose of Christ's coming to earth in the flesh was to put away sin. His reappearance in heavenly glory will complete the salvation of all the redeemed. Whereas His first coming concentrated on the plan of dealing with sin, His second coming will be without consideration of sin; that has been taken care of. His reappearance will be focused on gathering the redeemed into the folds of glory. It will accommodate the saints and bring judgment upon the ungodly.

Our faith has sufficient evidence to believe confidently in this promise of Christ's return. His acts of providence lead up to that final deliverance from the very presence of sin. Those who trust and look for this great event will not be disappointed. We now look for His coming with confident expectation of the fullest realization of God's saving grace.

Salvation Necessitates Human Response

If thou shalt confess with thy mouth the Lord Jesus, and shalt believe in thine heart that God hath raised him from the dead, thou shalt be saved. For with the heart man believeth unto righteousness; and with the mouth confession is made unto salvation. For whosoever shall call upon the name of the Lord shall be saved—Romans 10:9, 10, 13.

This passage constitutes a formula of human response to the call of God. It is expressed in the Gospel of Jesus Christ. It points to various results of exercising faith. God's provision for redemption of people stands as the primary basis for humans to experience salvation. The first long step toward salvation is calling on the name of the Lord. The *whosoever* marks the universal opportunity to be saved. God makes no distinction on the basis of nationality, sex, privilege, or position (v. 12). To call on the name of the Lord includes various elements in human response such as a knowledge of God, repentance, faith, confession, and prayer.

1. Salvation Requires a Knowledge of God

Grace and peace be multiplied unto you through the knowledge of God and of Jesus our Lord. If after they have escaped the pollutions of the world through the knowledge of the Lord and Saviour Jesus Christ, they are again entangled therein, and overcome, the latter end is worse with them than the beginning. But grow in grace, and in the knowledge of our Lord and Saviour Jesus Christ.—II Peter 1:2; 2:20; 3:18.

The contexts of these passages express concern for the health of the church. The appeal for faithfulness is based on the initial Christian experience. They escaped the evils of the world through having had a knowledge of Jesus Christ, the Lord. To know the facts about the plan of redemption is essential to a genuine experience of salvation, but it is not enough. People cannot be saved without some knowledge also of its meaning. Today that knowledge is attained through the Word of God. A sinner must know that "God so loved the world, that he gave his only begotten Son, that whosoever believeth in him should not perish, but have everlasting life" (John 3:16).

2. Salvation Calls for Repentance

The Lord is not slack concerning his promise as some men count slackness; but is longsuffering to us-ward, not willing that any should perish but that all should come to repentance—II Peter 3:9.

The meaning of repentance, as set forth in the Scriptures, can hardly be overstated. The proclamation of the Gospel has a major focus on the importance of reaching the point of being sorry for having sinned. The pastoral concern of Peter, as expressed in the text above, is God's call to repentance as a way to be saved. Failure in this is to perish.

Repentance is a change of mind about the place of Christ in human experience. It emerges from a conviction brought about by the Holy Spirit. It is an acknowledgement that the way of indulging selfish desires and doings are wrong. As Paul put it, "I rejoice, not that ye were made sorry, but that ye sorrowed to repentance . . . after a godly manner" (II Corinthians 7:9). Contrition needs to be expressed by a voluntary change of behavior to the way of truth as expressed in the Scriptures.

3. Salvation Is Affirmed by Faith

Without faith it is impossible to please him [God]: for he that cometh to God must believe that he is, and that he is a rewarder of them that diligently seek him. Faith cometh by hearing and hearing by the Word of God. Therefore being justified by faith, we have peace with God through our Lord Jesus Christ—Hebrews 11:6; Romans 10:17; 5:1.

Faith is a fundamental aspect of the human response to the divine invitation to be saved. Christ emphasized faith as an important step toward salvation. It goes beyond the point of believing to an assent of the heart and mind to the subsequent claims of Christ. A person in coming to God must know Jesus as Saviour and also as Lord. It means having a diligent desire for a continuing personal relationship with Him, giving Him worship and service. By receiving Christ in this manner, a deliberate choice is made to live in obedience to the Word of God. That relationship is established on the basis of knowing who He is and what He has done. The whole experience of salvation depends upon such faith.

4. Salvation Is Expressed by Confession

Every spirit that confesseth that Jesus Christ is come in the flesh is of God. Whosoever shall confess me before men, him shall the Son of man also confess before the angels of God. Every tongue should confess that Jesus Christ is Lord, to the glory of God the Father. Wherefore . . . as ye have always obeyed, not as in my presence only, but now much more in my absence, work out your own salvation with fear and trembling. If we confess our sins, he [God] is faithful and just to forgive us our sins, and to cleanse us from all unrighteousness—I John 4:2b; Luke 12:8; Philippians 2:11, 12; I John 1:9.

Repentance represents the heart's desire to be saved. Confession accompanies the penitence with intentions to follow Christ. It also has therapeutic value in relieving feelings of guilt and in making a commitment to forsake sin. That includes forsaking all that grieves God. The psalmist says, "I will declare mine iniquity; I will be sorry for my sin" (Psalm 38:18). The intention of a penitent person needs to be expressed with an "I will" that changes the whole outlook in life.

Confession is a verbal expression of sorrow for sins of the past including regrets for spiritual neglect in profession and action. It is an important aspect of working out our salvation with sober and sincere expressions of faith.

5. Salvation Is Made Real by Prayer

Lord, teach us to pray. And he said unto them, When ye pray, say, Our Father which art in heaven, Hallowed be thy name. Thy kingdom come. Thy will be done, as in heaven, so in earth. Give us day by day our daily bread. And forgive us our sins; for we also forgive every one that is indebted to us. And lead us not into temptation; but deliver us from evil. And I say unto you, Ask, and it shall be given you; seek, and ye shall find; knock, and it shall be opened unto you—Luke 11:1b, 2-4, 9.

It is a normal motivation for a penitent person to want to pray. With the initial response of faith, at the time of conversion a prayer of confession and supplication is sure to receive an answer from God. In asking for pardon, the person is expected to make a sincere expression of commitment to forsake sin.

In His Sermon on the Mount, Jesus made seeking the kingdom of God a priority in personal aspirations. This makes talking to God a matter of immediate urgency. The Prophet Jeremiah, in reporting God's message to Israel, repeated the condition of salvation, "Then shall ye call upon me [God], and ye shall go and pray unto me, and I will hearken unto you. And ye shall seek me, and find me when ye shall search for me with all your heart" (Jeremiah 29:12, 13).

Salvation Is a Continuing Experience

We . . . beseech you also that ye receive not the grace of God in vain. For he [Christ] saith, I have heard thee in a time accepted, and in the day of salvation have I succoured thee: behold, now is the accepted time; behold, now is the day of salvation—II Corinthians 6:1, 2.

The new life in God does not perpetuate itself automatically. There is always need for human response. This passage does not refer directly to the initial experience of salvation. It is an appeal to Christians to repeatedly accept the grace of God for victorious living.

1. Salvation Involves Discipline

Let us walk honestly, as in the day; not in rioting and drunkenness, not in chambering and wantonness, not in strife and envying. But put ye on the Lord Jesus Christ, and make not provision for the flesh, to fulfil the lusts thereof—Romans 13:13, 14.

The Christian walk, daily life, and conduct call for casting off the deeds and habits of the unbelieving world. A positive union with Christ results in disciplined behavior. Even as the indwelling Christ lifts us into the experience of His life, so He subdues in us the evil, sensual desires of the flesh. We make no opportunity for fleshly gratification. In Christ, then, we have not only been redeemed from all past sins, but we have also received divine grace to overcome present evils. The salvation experience gives power to live in the delights of spiritual victories.

2. Salvation Produces Righteous Behavior

Reckon ye also yourselves to be dead indeed unto sin, but alive unto God through Jesus Christ our Lord. Yield yourselves unto God, as those that are alive from the dead, and your members as instruments of righteousness unto God—Romans 6:11,13b.

In the section on divine acceptance, righteousness was explained as a declaration of God based on our faith. There it was coupled with justification, the declaration of our complete forgiveness and a new relationship with God. Righteousness, however, is not only a status, but a moral quality of behavior as well. It constitutes a conformity to God's will, a personal and active obedience to Christ, a compliance with the promptings of the Holy Spirit.

To count ourselves dead unto sin means we no longer give in to sinful desires. Being alive unto God through Christ Jesus, our bodies are no longer tools of wickedness. They are now tools of righteousness in the hands of God to accomplish His purposes. By a deliberate identification with Christ human faculties such as mind, will, and reason become instruments of righteousness unto God.

3. Salvation Includes Servanthood

Know ye not, that to whom ye yield yourselves servants to obey, his servants ye are to whom ye obey; whether of sin unto death, or of obedience unto righteousness? Now being made free from sin, and become servants to God, ye have your fruit unto holiness, and the end everlasting life—Romans 6:16,22.

In Christ human nature is transformed into a pattern of spiritual responses, a yielding in obedience to the Holy Spirit's promptings. "Being then made free from sin, ye became servants of righteousness" (Romans 6:18). In the practice of righteousness the believer becomes more like God. By accepting Christ as Lord and Saviour, Christian servanthood is focused on the principle of obedience. In following the leading of the Holy Spirit the believer's capacities are yielded for use in the kingdom of God. In the exercise of such obedience there is a resulting quality of life, the fruits of righteousness. The benefits of such obedience include holiness and everlasting life. Such lives are expressing holiness in testimony of God. Continuing service becomes a continuing opportunity to demonstrate the glory of God. It is truly a high honor to be His servant.

4. Salvation Engages Reconciliation

Therefore if any man be in Christ, he is a new creature: old things are passed away; behold all things are become new. And all things are of God, who hath reconciled us to himself by Jesus Christ, and hath given to us the ministry of reconciliation; to wit, that God was in Christ, reconciling the world unto himself, not imputing their trespasses unto them; and hath committed unto us the word of reconciliation—II Corinthians 5:17-19.

To "be in Christ" is to have had an experience of regeneration. Thereby one becomes a new creation. The former life with its secular standards of judgment are replaced by Biblical standards and new incentives. The person has a new nature. This new life indicates having been reconciled to God. That is accomplished by acceptance of the Lord Jesus Christ.

God's acceptance of a penitent person puts the believer into the position of giving testimony to the meaning of the Gospel of reconciliation. Adequate provision has been made to redeem lost souls. Having been reconciled to God, the believer's experience is extended to include a personal ministry of reconciliation in the world. One must seek to understand circumstances that create tensions and face any responsibility for involvement in such a problem. With a clear testimony of peace with God, one is ready to proclaim the word of reconciliation to others. The unbelieving world can be influenced by the promise of divine mercy and forgiveness.

5. Salvation Relies Upon Trust

We both labour and suffer reproach, because we trust in the living God, who is the Saviour of all men, specially of those that believe. Such trust have we through Christ to God-ward: not that we are sufficient of ourselves to think any thing as of ourselves; but our sufficiency is of God—I Timothy 4:10; II Corinthians 3:4,5.

Saving grace is available to all who trust in God and who identify themselves with Jesus Christ. By the act of faith the believer finds enough Christian sufficiency to live an abundant life. This trust whereby the believer first looked to Jesus for salvation is to be a continuing experience. Whereas provision for our redemption was made by the living God, the responsibility of claiming that grace rests with the believer. The old familiar song expressed it clearly, "When we walk with the Lord/ In the light of His Word,/ What a glory He sheds on our way!/ While we do His good will,/ He abides with us still,/ And with all who will trust and obey./ Trust and obey,/ For there's no other way/ To be happy in Jesus,/ But to trust and obey" (J. H. Sammis). We rely upon Jesus for direction, strength, and sustenance in all we face.

6. Salvation Involves Stewardship

Let a man so account of us, as of the ministers of Christ, and stewards of the mysteries of God. Moreover it is required in stewards, that a man be found faithful. Know ye not that your body is the temple of the Holy Ghost which is in you, which ye have of God, and ye are not your own? For ye are bought with a price: therefore glorify God in your body, and in your spirit, which are God's—I Corinthians 4:1,2; 6:19,20.

Not only is a Christian a minister of Christ, but he is also a steward of the mysteries (secret things) of God. It is required that he be faithful in performing the will of God. In that relationship the believer is to use the resources given to him for the fulfillment of divine purposes.

The Christian is not his own. God has placed His Spirit in us to provide a Representative from heaven to guide us in the performance of Christian duty. In the stewardship of life, our bodies and spirits (physical and spiritual beings), which are God's, are to be used to promote the interests of His kingdom. The benefits of living for God put meaning into our Christian profession. This comes about by dedication of our talents, by promoting the Gospel of Christ, by tithing of our financial income to support Christian activities, and by helping people in need.

Salvation Is Sustained by Christian Action

Thanks be to God, which giveth us the victory through our Lord Jesus Christ. Therefore, my beloved brethren, be ye steadfast, unmoveable, always abounding in the work of the Lord, forasmuch as ye know that your labour is not in vain in the Lord—I Corinthians 15:57,58.

These verses come at the close of a dramatic portrayal of life after death. They represent both present and eternal victory over sin. The day of Christ's return is anticipated. That will be the fulfillment of our living hope. It is obvious that preparation for that occasion calls for faithfulness in human action. It means a close adherence to the professed faith and a diligent performance of Christian duty.

1. Salvation Is Sustained by Firm Commitment

You, that were sometimes alienated and enemies in your mind by wicked works, yet now hath he [Jesus Christ] reconciled in the body of his flesh through death, to present you holy and unblameable and unreproveable in his sight: If ye continue in the faith grounded and settled, and be not moved away from the hope of the gospel—Colossians 1:21-23a.

This reflection on the marvelous grace of God points to our own reconciliation with Him. It introduces God's intention to achieve in His children holiness in this life and hope for heaven. It represents the plan and action of God who has made redemption available to all who come to Christ in sincere faith. That prescribes the condition to have a personal and prevailing commitment to Christ.

The status of reconciliation and peace with God is kept in effect by being committed wholeheartedly to a firm faith in Christ. It also means maintaining a settled conviction and practice of the teachings of the Gospel. Added to these elements of experience is a vital hope in the promised future elements of salvation.

2. Salvation Is Sustained by Faithfulness

Brethren, I declare unto you the gospel . . . wherein ye stand; by which also ye are saved, if ye keep in memory what I [Paul] preached unto you . . . how that Christ died for our sins . . . and that he rose again the third day—I Corinthians 15:1-4a.

This passage is taken from a context of truth about the death and resurrection of Jesus Christ. It calls attention to the kind of life that sustains salvation. The anticipated resurrection of the saints gives meaning to human response to the marvelous provision of redemption. We stand in the Gospel and we are urged to hold fast to the Word of God. We are expected to adopt its truth and practice its outline of obedience. Faithfulness in this regard sustains the benefits of being saved.

We know the crucifixion of Jesus is the basis of forgiveness of sin. The power of His resurrection vitalizes the Christian walk. Being loyal in acceptance of Christ's lordship keeps faith alive and active. "When ye received the Word of God which ye heard of us, ye received it not as the word of men, but as it is in truth, the word of God, which effectually worketh also in you that believe" (I Thessalonians 2:13).

3. Salvation Is Sustained by Union With Christ

I am the true vine and my Father is the husbandman. Every branch in me that beareth not fruit he taketh away. . . . Now ye are clean through the word which I have spoken unto you. Abide in me, and I in you. As the branch cannot bear fruit of itself, except it abide in the vine; no more can ye, except ye abide in me. I am the vine, ye are the branches. He that abideth in me, and I in him, the same bringeth forth much fruit: for without me ye can do nothing—John 15:1-5.

Christ is preeminent in the total plan of redemption. The illustration in this passage has a direct application to the offers of salvation. To abide in Him is to rely upon His presence and to keep life open to His will. It is a matter of constant identification with the Word, to which we have ready access. When the aim of Christ is ours, when His principles control our actions, when His message becomes our motivation, and when His vision becomes our goal, we are abiding in Him.

This union with Christ as branches of the True Vine puts into effect such characteristics as discipline, prayer, love, and obedience. The life of Christ is thereby manifested in the believer, and the purposes of God are accomplished. The fruit, benefits of salvation, are the result of this relationship with Christ in daily living.

4. Salvation Is Sustained by Truth

Jesus said, *If ye continue in my word, then are ye my disciples indeed; and ye shall know the truth, and the truth shall make you free*—John 8:31b, 32.

Jesus was teaching in the temple when some of His audience "believed *on* Him," that is, accepted Him in faith. To these people Jesus explained the true nature of discipleship and the meaning of being set free. He based these points on a continuing conformity to His Word. Salvation is sustained by repeated exposure to and application of the truth. A beginner's faith needs a progressive commitment to the truth.

Discipleship means believing in Christ and living by what He has taught. Freedom means having a knowledge of what is true about Christ and living in the benefits of believing that truth. It requires more than an emotional response and more than a mere profession. It calls for full conformity to the Word of truth and commitment to its meaning. This relationship with Christ provides a progressive support to the experience of salvation. It offers freedom through forgiveness of sin and deliverance from it.

5. Salvation Is Sustained by Steadfastness

Christ as a son over his own house; whose house are we, if we hold fast the confidence and the rejoicing of the hope firm unto the end. For we are made partakers of Christ, if we hold the beginning of our confidence steadfast unto the end—Hebrews 3:6, 14.

Let us hold firmly to the confidence we had in Christ at the beginning of our Christian experience. That is a condition that inspires loyalty to Him and hope in the promise of His return. It pertains to the original faith placed in Him for salvation. That status is firmly established by personal prevailing commitment to Christ. Union with Him provides incentives to loyalty and confidence in the purposes of God. A confident relationship first established at the time of conversion continues on the basis of an earnest desire to continue in the will of God. Reality in the Christian race relies upon that kind of personal commitment.

We base our hope on divine promises related to the total scope of redemption. Constancy and steadfastness in believing and behavior are essential to sustain our relationship with Christ. Even as we persist in our confidence in Him, so He continues in His supply of grace to us.

6. Salvation Is Sustained by Integrity

If ye through the Spirit do mortify the deeds of the body, ye shall live. For as many as are led by the Spirit of God, they are the sons of God—Romans 8:13b, 14.

This condition upon which salvation is sustained rests upon human action motivated and infiltrated by the Holy Spirit. The feelings and desires related to the believer's body are made subject to the Spirit's influence. The inclinations of the flesh and all forms of carnal desire are brought under control, not by mere self-assertion, but by reliance upon the grace of God. When the deeds of the body are thus mortified, the believer's life is characterized by holiness and happiness. "To be spiritually minded is life and peace" (Romans 8:6), a life led by the Holy Spirit in fulfillment of divine purposes.

The integrity of the new life in Christ is expressed in actual victory over sinful fleshly desires. With the Holy Spirit in control of personal desires and actions, the believer's body is quickened and invigorated by special divine life. Any attempt to do this by human strength alone is futile. We rely on the grace of God to support personal commitment.

7. Salvation Is Sustained by Prayer

Be careful for nothing; but in every thing by prayer and supplication with thanksgiving let your requests be made known unto God. And the peace of God, which passeth all understanding, shall keep your hearts and minds through Christ Jesus. Continue in prayer, and watch in the same with thanksgiving—Philippians 4:6,7; Colossians 4:2.

This passage addresses the common problem of anxiety (being "careful"). An answer is found in sincere and confident prayer. When requests are made to God, they are to be submitted in the context of expressed gratitude. With freedom from care, Christian experience is characterized by an abiding and abounding peace. That sustains faith. It keeps the heart and mind in vital and perpetual touch with God.

When you pray, hold God in deep respect. He is ready to share His wisdom. "If any of you lack wisdom, let him ask of God, that giveth to all men liberally, and upbraideth not; and it shall be given him. But let him ask in faith, nothing wavering" (James 1:5, 6a). He is also ready to use His providence to benefit His children. To address Him as Father requires genuine filial experience. Children of God engage in prayer daily and perpetually, expressing praise and adoration in intimate communion. Prayer is motivated by commitment to divine will and purposes. It is also a great weapon with which to resist the enemy and overcome temptation. It is indeed an effective instrument to sustain the experience of salvation.

Salvation Is a Way of Life

Master, we know that thou art true, and teachest the way of God in truth. These men are the servants of the most high God, which show unto us the way of salvation—Matthew 22:16; Acts 16:17.

Members of the early church were called people of "the way" (Acts 9:2). As Paul preached and taught about the Holy Ghost and laid hands on new believers, they received the Spirit. Various people whose hearts were hardened against the truth about Jesus, spoke evil of the "way." Later it was reported that unbelievers were stirred up against "the way" (Acts 19:9, 23). As we have seen in previous discussions, the term is used also to identify various aspects of "the way" such as "the way of peace," "the way of righteousness," "the way of truth," "new and living way," etc. This justifies our use of this word in identifying the descriptive phrases in the following paragraphs.

1. Salvation Is the Way of Christ

I am the way, the truth, and the life. In him [Christ] dwelleth all the fulness of the Godhead bodily. And ye are complete in him, which is the head of all principality and power—John 14:6; Colossians 2:9, 10.

When Thomas became eager to know more about how to go to the Father's house (heaven), he asked Jesus, "How can we know the way?" Basically he inquired about the way to be saved. Jesus replied, "I am the way." That expression became the simple designation of Christians in the early church. They were people of "the way." Christ is the true and only way to the Father; we are invited to follow in His steps.

The idea of Christ being the Way is an important principle which is expanded in meaning by the designations *truth* and *life*. In this context Christ presents Himself as the way to God and to eternal life. As stated above, He is the only means by which a penitent sinner can be saved.

Truth sums up what can be known about God and Christ. Trust in Christ is derived from having heard the Word of truth, which is the Gospel of salvation. The truth of the Gospel points to the provision made by Christ's death and resurrection. Having accepted His saving grace, the Christian is marked as belonging to Christ by the promised Holy Spirit. He becomes an assurance of our spiritual inheritance. His indwelling presence is an initial deposit of eternal glory (Ephesians 1:13,14). The believer is thereby sanctified and enlightened to worship God now in spirit and in truth.

Jesus, as the *life*, focuses on what He imparts to the believer by His indwelling presence. As the eternal One, He is not only the Source of eternal life but also is the Giver of life. He came that we might have life but also to have it in overflowing fulness (John 10:10). His life gives light for all mankind. That light identifies the meaning of life in Him. With Christ in the center of life-giving action, those who believe in Him possess eternal values. Persons who have a warm personal and perpetual relationship with Christ have full confidence in the truth and great contentment in everlasting life.

2. Salvation Is the Way of God

A certain Jew named Apollos . . . an eloquent man and mighty in the scriptures [O.T.], came to Ephesus. This man was instructed in the way of the Lord . . . knowing only the baptism of John. And he began to speak boldly in the synagogue: whom when Aquila and Priscilla had heard, they took him unto them, and expounded unto him the way of God more perfectly—Acts 18:24-26.

Apollos was one of the outstanding persons of leadership in the early church. His exceptional ability was enhanced by believing in Jesus and by knowing of His life and teachings. But Apollos had not been taught about the significance of Jesus' death, of His resurrection, and of His ascension. Neither did he know of the Pentecostal gift of the Spirit. Aquila and Priscilla, however, told him the full truth about Christ and about the way of God.

In our time there are persons who miss being instructed in the way of God. They may have responded to the call of repentance; they may have been told to exercise social justice; and they may have been led to a position of public integrity. But that is not enough to fulfill the expectations of the Christian life. They need an inner change of heart. With that they can be led to understand the full Gospel. After yielding themselves to Christ as Lord of their lives, they can walk in the way of God and enjoy the "fulness of the blessing of the Gospel of Christ."

3. Salvation Is the Way of the Holy Spirit

It is expedient for you [Jesus says] that I go away: for if I go not away, the Comforter will not come unto you; but if I depart, I will send him unto you. When he, the Spirit of truth, is come, he will guide you into all truth. He shall glorify me—John 16:7, 13a, 14a.

God has planned to have the Holy Spirit meet human spiritual needs. The Spirit reproves the world of sin and convicts sinners of their spiritual needs. He makes people aware of the effects of present and future judgment.

The Spirit functions in the life of a believer by giving guidance in matters that affect Christian experience and witness. He applies the grace of God to our daily behavior. He keeps alive in us an awareness of God's will to live and serve in the name of Jesus. Through the Spirit the power of God keeps working in us.

A careful reading of the entire Gospel of John reveals in large measure the function of the Spirit. He generates eternal life and sustains it through the years of believing. He motivates worship, provides quickening power, and produces a spiritual overflow of joy and peace. He indwells the believer to provide providential guidance.
"Holy Spirit, faithful Guide,
Ever near the Christian's side,
Gently lead us by the hand,
Pilgrims in a desert land."
—Marcus Wells

This intimate relationship with the Spirit is a perpetual reality in all faithful believers. Our assurance of salvation deepens as the Holy Spirit works in our hearts to exalt Jesus Christ and to perpetuate faith in Him.

4. Salvation Is the Way of Obedience

Wherefore, my beloved, as ye have always obeyed, not as in my presence only, but now much more in my absence, work out your own salvation with fear and trembling. For it is God which worketh in you both to will and to do of his good pleasure—Philippians 2:12, 13.

The context of this passage is an appeal to "let this mind be in you, which was also in Christ Jesus" (v. 5) who "took upon him the form of a servant" (v. 7), and "humbled himself, and became obedient unto death, even the death of the cross" (v. 8). Thus, the pattern of obedience is in Christ whose commitment was focused on God's purpose for His life. Conformity to His way is the key to Christian behavior. Our obedience is based on personal commitment which finds its expression in doing the will of God. It is God who touches the inner life with promptings to invest energy in fulfilling His purposes. The believer submits to divine providence for the glory of God.

Christians are called to apply Biblical principles in their daily walk. Jesus set an example of servanthood for His followers. We are also called to an investment in Christian witness. This is not a matter of working to earn salvation. Rather, it is a response to God's working in us both to will and to do of His good pleasure.

5. Salvation Is the Way of Transformation

I beseech you therefore, brethren, by the mercies of God, that ye present your bodies a living sacrifice, holy, acceptable unto God, which is your reasonable service. And be not conformed to this world: but be ye transformed by the renewing of your mind, that ye may prove what is that good, and acceptable, and perfect, will of God—Romans 12:1, 2.

Salvation introduces a life-style that expresses the will of God. This passage has an urgent appeal to all who are called Christians. It is based upon the mercies of God. He honors our justification in Christ and respects those who are sanctified by the Holy Spirit. We are called to present our bodies as living sacrifices to honor God. In our human experience we are expected to show how to live for Christ.

Transformed living (following regeneration) accepts the divine pattern of behavior. It motivates conduct that is controlled by divine principles. With the love of Christ constraining the inner life, the outward expression of faith overcomes worldliness. The Christian therefore is not conformed to the practices of the world. In belonging to God the believer avoids being controlled by worldly standards, selfish motives, and sinful impulses. The will of God rules out compromises with the world in business transactions, in social behavior, in appearance, and in material accumulations. The total manner of life bears the marks of transformation in which the mind of Christ prevails, and a newness of life follows. It is a way by which we do those things that are pleasing to God.

2.

Assurance Involves a Doctrine of Experience

These things have I written unto you that believe on the name of the Son of God; that ye may know that ye have eternal life, and that ye may believe on the name of the Son of God—I John 5:13.

Assurance Pertains to Certainty of Salvation

God hath from the beginning chosen you to salvation through sanctification of the Spirit and belief of the truth—II Thessalonians 2:13b.

The answer to the question, "How can I know I am saved?" is the meaning of assurance. To know that one is saved is a matter of ascertaining the conditions of salvation as revealed in the Scriptures. It pertains to our personal relationship with God. Assurance of salvation is a truth that lies close to the surface throughout the New Testament. The note of certainty is everywhere present. The Gospels were written to put an end to doubt and anxiety. The epistle writers had a strong passion to promote the certainty of faith. People everywhere who believe the Bible is the inspired Word of God find in its message a great note of certainty.

Assurance is based upon a definite knowledge of the truth which pertains to God's promises in relation to salvation. It is accompanied by a clear-cut experience in spiritual realities. The assured Christian knows he has forgiveness of sins. He understands that Christ has made for him complete reconciliation with God. He is conscious of a satisfactory personal relationship with Him. He has confidence both in the trustworthiness of God and in the reality of his own experience of faith. Richard Watson says it is "a comfortable persuasion, or conviction of our justification and adoption, arising out of the Spirit's inward and direct testimony."[1] When sin is forgiven, when a new nature is given, when communion with God is restored, the believer is by some means assured of it. Instead of fear, anxiety, or doubt, the person has peace of mind and satisfaction in his soul. He has a sense of reality in his acceptance with God. He knows he is saved.

Salvation is designated in the Scriptures by a variety of terms. The most common among them is "eternal life." Others meaning essentially the same thing are "know God," "abide in Him," "born of God." While these terms represent different aspects of the experience of salvation, they all pertain to a certain quality of life. Assurance is knowing that one possesses eternal life.

The apostles were utterly certain of their salvation. They were sure that Christ had risen from the dead and that they were partaking of His life. But very early in the history of the church Satan created doubts, raised suspicions, and set up prejudices among the believers. Then the power of the church was dissipated.[2] So long as they kept alive the consciousness of the risen and living Christ and maintained the note of assurance and confidence, the cause of Christ grew and the church enlarged its borders. But through the course of its history, evil influences destroyed the confidence of faith and the certainty of salvation so that the church became weaker and less effective in its witness.

The doctrine of salvation as held by the Roman Catholic Church is very directly related to the sacrament of penance and of priestly absolution. The doctrine of assurance was lost to them because they neglected those Scriptures which uphold the direct communication of the Holy Spirit to the believer. The reformers revived the precious doctrine. Both Luther and Calvin used strong expressions on different points, implying that one who lacks personal assurance cannot be regarded as a true believer. Calvin, believing that the Christian is not always free from doubts and perplexities, made allowance for feelings of assurance to increase and decrease in proportion to the strength and weakness of faith. He was firm, however, in holding that true faith allows no doubts respecting final salvation.[3] Believing that assurance is of the essence of faith and that, therefore, all believers must have assurance, these reformers insisted that one could not be a believer without knowing it. They believed it required a special revelation from God, which every true believer must certainly have. Rejoicing in the assurance of salvation was a tower of spiritual strength. This Christian certitude was a great factor in making the reformers irresistible in their advance with Christian truth.

The Anabaptists in their vigorous protest against all forms of licentious and fruitless living made much of the importance of genuineness in Christian faith. Their view of Christianity laid stress upon righteous conduct. Their writings made copious use of Scriptures that prescribe Christian duty and personal behavior. They were concerned about both correctness of doctrine and holiness of life. They used these elements of faith and standards of life to test the genuineness of Christian experience. An example of this approach is found in Menno Simons' treatise on Faith. He set before the reader passages from the New Testament "as a clear mirror, in which you may view yourselves, and see whether you are believing Christians."[4] Menno submits the following tests of genuineness: (1) Being born of the Word you will have "no more pride, unchastity, avarice, hatred and envy in you." (2) Having repented truly, being baptized rightly, having your heart circumcised, having died to sin and risen in Christ you have new life. (3) Refusal to keep the commandments shows that "you hate the commands of the Lord and have not his faith." (4) A willingness to forsake all for Christ and to take up the cross daily in self-denial, to "enter with Christ on the way of suffering" is evidence of being on the narrow way. (5) When you overcome lusts and carnal ways and "trample them under foot, through faith, then thank God, fight piously, watch and pray." (6) A personal trust in God's providential care "is a true evidence that you have the Word of the Lord." (7) Sincere belief in Jesus Christ is further evidence that your old carnal mind has become a regenerated, spiritual mind.

Leaders of the Anabaptists held that one may approach God in full confidence of having a genuine Christian faith.

A later development of this doctrine found form in the Pietistic movement during the seventeenth and eighteenth centuries. The Pietists sought the assurance of faith (or of salvation) in experience too much apart from the Word of God. Instead of relying upon the promises of the Gospel, they depended almost wholly upon inner experience—a knowledge of experience became the touchstone of faith rather than a knowledge of the Word of God. This led to a form of assurance which shifted away from the true standards of divine revelation. So, in our search for Christian evidence, instead of obtaining assurance from states of feeling, we rely more upon fact as revealed in the Word of God.

In the rise of Modernism, the supernatural was discredited. This means that Modernists discount miracles of grace. They do not ask whether the Christian has experienced a supernatural change. Since they question the inspiration of the Bible and regard its message reliable only insofar as it can be confirmed by reason, they are indifferent to matters pertaining to the doctrine of assurance.

It is the purpose of this book to recapture the truth of the Scriptures relating to the doctrine of assurance and to develop a Christian philosophy of experience that is both reasonable and Biblical.

Assurance Copes With Doubt

Whom [Jesus Christ] having not seen, ye love; in whom, though now ye see him not, yet believing, ye rejoice with joy unspeakable and full of glory: Receiving the end of your faith, even the salvation of your souls—I Peter 1:8,9.

Assurance is needed *to give a sense of reality to faith.* While enduring bodily infirmities or seasons of unusual temptation, the Christian sometimes needs a reassurance of faith. Unusual experiences may raise questions or even doubts about spiritual relationships. At such times, when faith is under test, it takes a firm persuasion to sustain the believing soul.

The believer who has a settled conviction about his relation to Christ is *fortified against temptation.* The devil, knowing the strength of an assured soul, begins to work subtly and secretly behind the scenes of life, first to break down confidence, and then to frame seductions that bring about moral and spiritual collapse. A person who is in doubt about his standing with God is an easy mark for satanic aims. The person who lacks assurance when the clouds of discontent gather is likely to become unsettled and to waver in his faith. If the darkness of discouragement thickens about him, he loses courage. If the storms of disappointment break around him, he inclines to yield to temptation. One in whom distrust, fear, anxiety, or murmuring prevail is helpless to cope with evil. But the believer who has the full assurance of faith is not so easily overthrown. He is equipped with strength of purpose and a sense of honor to resist temptation.

Assurance of salvation sustains *happiness in Christian experience.* A humble but firm sense of acceptance with God is a great source of personal delight. This idea of assurance is essentially bound up with our ideas of God and of His attitudes toward us. It has a direct bearing upon our daily religious life. It has so much to do with our happiness that no Christian can afford to ignore it. Continual uncertainty in matters of any kind leads to unrest, and unrest is altogether opposed to the promises of Christ.

The blood of Christ has been shed to give the heart rest; confidence in His atonement brings peace, joy, and rejoicing. To go forward in life with freedom and hope requires firm ground on which to tread. James Hastings asserts, "To assure the conscience of pardon, to vanquish the fear of extinction in death, or the fear of awful judgment beyond, to reach the depth of man's spirit, the seat of his misery, by an effectual assurance of reconciliation, demands the direct and healing touch of a divine life-giving hand, the direct voice of the Almighty Consoler. This requires a distinctly revealed 'covenant,' not a guess, or a hope [—so] proceeding from man, but an 'oath and a promise' of God; not a human peradventure, but a clear and distinct revelation of the redeeming love which apprehends us in Christ."[5]

Assurance is an *essential qualification for Christian service.* Who will give himself to sacrificing labors in the kingdom but one who believes intensely in Jesus Christ? Where there is no sense of certainty, life is without full meaning and purpose. Christian service requires a positive and vigorous approach. Not only must the servant of the Lord know the facts which constitute the story of the Gospel, but he must also know the reality of personal experience with Christ. On this point Louis Berkhof adds, "If his gait is halting and uncertain, if his arms are unsteady, if his eye is not clear and true, and if he is lacking in confidence, he will not be able to do his best for the Captain of his salvation. But if he stands in the assurance of faith, he will march to the battle with confidence, will occupy a strong position, will aim with precision, and will fight with the strength that comes from the confident expectation of victory."[6] If a man is to live the Christian life happily, there may be no guessing about his salvation. If he is to serve Christ effectively, he dare not hesitate to recommend the message and method of redemption.

The testimony to the Gospel must be proved by a life of certainties. Any doubts or anxieties regarding personal relation with God tend to raise questions in the mind of the unbeliever regarding the soundness of the Gospel message. If we want to testify with power we must be convinced of the truth ourselves before we will urge others to accept it. Faith stands for life and power; it professes to bring hope and immortality. To believe in these factors half-heartedly, or to have no sense of certainty about them, is to concede defeat. It admits silently that religion has degenerated into an empty form. G. G. Findlay makes a strong appeal for more dynamic Christian leadership when he says, "Greatly do we need, like the Asian disciples of Paul and John, to 'assure our hearts' before God. With death confronting us, with the hideous evil of the world oppressing us; when the air is laden with the contagion of sin; when the faith of the strongest wears the cast of doubt; when the word of promise shines dimly through the haze of an all-encompassing skepticism and a hundred voices say, in mockery or grief, Where is now thy God? When the world proclaims us lost, our faith refuted, our Gospel obsolete and useless—then is the time for the Christian assurance to recover its first energy and to rise again in radiant strength from the heart of the church, from the depths of its mystic life where it is hid with Christ in God."[7]

Assurance of salvation *lays a firm ground for victorious living* and is really essential to a thoroughly Christian character. If the Christian life is to have fullness of joy and beauty of character, it must have singleness of purpose, entire trust in the Master, and consecration to His service.[8] The person who loves God with all his soul, who trusts Christ with all his mind, and who obeys the Spirit with all his strength will be certain about his experience, character, and destiny.

Assurance is the first result in the Christian life.

"Who comes to God an inch through doubtings dim,
In blazing light God will advance a mile to him."[9]

Because much of the failure in spiritual experience is due to the absence of assurance, it is important that initial experience with Christ include a definite persuasion of salvation. Imagine children who doubt their most evident parentage, or heirs who hesitate to receive their inheritance, or a bride who after the ceremony doubts the reality of her marriage. A similar attitude in Christian experience is no less absurd. Such doubts regarding salvation easily, and sometimes quickly, lead to indifference, anxiety, unkindness, disappointment, sorrow, and rebellion.

The person who is confident of his standing with God, who has wholly committed himself to God, and who shares the joy of salvation can more easily forego sensual indulgence and the pursuit of worldly ambitions. If he had only a dim probability of attaining eternal rest, if his relation with Christ were only a vague dream, or if his prospects for delightful intercourse with God lay in a doubtful future, his desire to overcome sin would be very weak. Christian morality finds its strength in certainty of reconciliation with God, in an overflowing gladness for the forgiveness of sins, and in being certain that the deed is right. We quote Findlay again, who says, "It was this confidence of present salvation that made the church irresistible. With its foundation secure, the house of life can be steadily and calmly built. Under the shelter of the full assurance of faith, in the sunshine of God's love felt in the heart, all spiritual virtues bloom and flourish. But with a faith hesitant and distracted, a faith that is certain of no doctrine in the creed and cannot plant a firm foot anywhere, nothing prospers in the soul or in the church."[10]

Assurance Rests on Divine Approval

He [God] hath made us accepted in the beloved. In whom [Christ] we have redemption through his blood, the forgiveness of sins, according to the riches of his grace—Ephesians 1:6b, 7.

Some people are not sure what to expect in assurance of salvation. They do not know how to identify the elements of experience that constitute assurance. They inquire, "How can one know he is saved?" Is it the result of a purely intellectual assent to truth or does accepting the truth produce a certain recognizable emotional state? Are there outward evidences or does one depend entirely upon inward impression? Is it the realization of a present state of soul or does it refer to the hope for some future blessing? Is one fully conscious of it or does it pertain to a condition of which one is not aware? Does one just believe it is true or are there some tangible evidences to examine? Does one look only into the realm of experience or are there other factors involved? Answers to these questions will help to understand the nature of Christian assurance.

There are certain facts we know about God and about His plan for redeeming man. An acceptance of all truth as fact is an *intellectual* process. When the mind is convinced of truth, the Christian has a basis upon which to rest his faith. He is persuaded of the reality of his experience by the knowledge he has of the facts available. Being convinced of the fact and knowing the nature of the fact gives ground for certainty.

Of what then in the realm of experience can we be sure? The knowledge of what facts enables us to rejoice in salvation? It is knowing the forgiveness of sins, knowing our acceptance with God, knowing our adoption into the family of God, knowing our position with Christ, knowing our possession of eternal life, knowing our privileges in Christ, and knowing the promise of an eternal inheritance. Above all, we are certain about God, the Object of our faith. We know, too, that the Bible is His instrument of communication; in it we have the revelation of His will and the statement of His promises.

The *emotional state* resulting from the persuasion that what is promised in the Word of God has been given to us with kind intent makes up another important factor in personal assurance. When a person believes that the gifts of God's love are for him, when he has by faith made use of them in his own experience, he finds deep soul satisfaction. The comfort, the confidence, and the joy one receives from such knowledge adds great meaning to his friendship with God.

Matters of which we are convinced in our minds are supported by the evidence which emerges from the things about which we are persuaded emotionally. The elements of personal assurance go beyond our merely believing that there is an adequate plan of salvation. Assurance embraces the element of trust; we feel confident about the One who has made faith possible. Such a state of feeling overcomes fears and doubts pertaining to the Word and accepts without reservation the promises it reveals. When the mind rests calmly convinced of the truth, and the heart relies in full confidence upon God, the believer is undisturbed by winds of false doctrine or storms of doubt. The consciousness of love to God, of trust and confidence in Him, of reverence and childlike respect for Him, is conducive to blessed communion with Him; it becomes a source of joy in obedient service to Him.[11] It enables him to say he knows he is saved; he knows he has eternal life.

Assurance is derived from a unique form of *inward impression*. Just as one can say he is sure of himself, so he can also say he is sure of his spiritual life. In the varied circumstances of natural life the question arises, often unconsciously, "How will this affect me?" No one doubts the self which raises that question in the realm of natural consequences. One can raise the same question about spiritual issues—"How will this affect my spiritual life?" This assumption of spiritual experience is an inner testimony yielding evidence of the reality of eternal life.

The Holy Spirit is the primary agent who brings this impression to the inner life. He so works upon the soul by His immediate influence—and this may be an unexplainable operation—as to produce a sense of moral and spiritual satisfaction. The heart rest which one finds through being fully satisfied that his transgressions are forgiven is an element of assurance. It is what Wesley describes as "an inward impression on the soul, whereby the Spirit of God directly witnesses to my spirit, that I am a child of God; that Jesus Christ hath loved me and given Himself for me; and that all my sins are blotted out, and I, even I, am reconciled to God."[12] The work of the Spirit is certainly recognizable.

The Scriptures say the believer is saved. The emphasis in salvation is neither upon future tense nor past tense but upon the present. Salvation is not an attainment to be achieved eventually through human effort, but is a present spiritual condition derived from the gloriously accomplished fact of redemption. This emphasis upon present reality occurs again and again in such statements as, "we **have** redemption through his blood." In every epistle there are expressions of assurance which denote the present tense of possession, such as "are," "you have," "hath," and "is." At no place is there any hint of a "hope so" or "perhaps so." There is in the whole of the New Testament a tenor of rejoicing in present experience. The epistles are addressed to people whose good standing with God is assured.

There has been a great deal of controversy as to whether it is possible for a person to be saved and not know it. We will not attempt to explore arguments for the views involved. We feel safe to assume, however, that a believer may be without the full assurance of faith and be saved. It would be a case in which a person is aware of an experience which he is unable to name. Nevertheless, whatever of Christian experience he is able to recognize must be the result of supernatural forces; there is no real salvation without the work of divine grace.

The presence of the Spirit in the life of the believer constitutes the most universal consciousness of sonship. The sense of divine indwelling, the assuring signs of divine leading, and the work of divine grace are all conscious experience. They are evidences of divine blessing.

Assurance Is Based on Scripture

Jesus said, *Search the scriptures; for in them ye think ye have eternal life: and they are they which testify of me*—John 5:39.

The certainty with which the apostles wrote concerning the death and resurrection of Christ points to the basic principles of assurance. The resurrection of Christ in particular certifies that satisfactory atonement has been made for our sins. This has "perfected for ever them that are sanctified." All who are united with Christ in His "endless life" are standing in a favored position; the ground of their assurance is permanently established.

There is no presumption in a sincere believer who says, "My sins are all forgiven," or who says, "I have eternal life." In the written testimony of God we have a promise to everyone that believes, saying that he has eternal life (John 3:36). The Scriptures plainly indicate the Christian is "justified from all things" (Acts 13:39). R. A. Torrey says, "It is the blood of Christ that makes us safe; it is the Word of God that makes us sure."[13] It is this Word of God which enables the believer to know his standing with God. As in the case from the passage of Acts 13:39, the believer can know that he is justified from all things if he knows that he believes in Jesus Christ. His assurance rests upon the simple statements of the Word of God.

Assurance depends largely upon a faith that relies upon the Word of God. It accepts the testimony of God's written Word. Too often people expect the Spirit to give them an inward testimony before they are willing to accept the outward testimony of the Word. This reversing of God's order has created a great deal of difficulty for troubled souls. One great purpose for which the New Testament is written is to give peace and joy in the Holy Ghost. This means it is not so much what we feel but what is recorded. It is not so much what our awareness has been, but what has been written. An unquestioned acceptance of the Word forms the sure foundation for our assurance of salvation.

The basis of Christian assurance is not limited to the objective promises of God. There is also the inward testimony of experience in the Holy Spirit. The Christian who exercises a good conscience and who produces the fruit of the Spirit has evidence concurring with that of the Word. Our relations with the Lord are personal, and therefore we look for evidence in the realm of experience. While we do not depend on our feeling for the initial evidence, the emotions of experience provide complementary evidence.

Our assurance of salvation is capable of intelligent investigation. Although it is superhuman in its nature and has its source in God, it may be vindicated by intellectual processes known to us by looking within ourselves. It is reasonable to believe that God's character, especially His love, does not allow Him to withhold from His children any information that would improve their relationship to Him as children.

Although assurance cannot be explained by natural considerations alone, there are certain tangible evidences which appear on the surface of human experience, making it both reasonable and real. When one has done well, he has a sense of satisfaction; when he has done evil, he has a sense of fear and guilt. Such a testimony of the conscience is unmistakably clear in acts of love for neighbors, in purity of life and thought, in personal behavior, and in the exercise of worship toward God. Our own spirit agrees with such testimony to what we do and to what we are.[14] Richard Watson's quotation from Thomas Scott's Commentary carries this idea further: "The Holy Spirit, by producing in believers the tempers and affections of children, as described in the Scriptures, most manifestly attests their adoption into God's family. This is not done by any voice, or by an immediate revelation, or impluse, or merely by any text brought to the mind (for all these are equivocal and delusory) but by coinciding with the testimony of their own consciences, as to their uprightness in embracing the Gospel, and giving themselves up to the service of God. So that, while they are examining themselves as to the reality of their conversion, and find Scriptural evidence of it, the Holy Spirit, from time to time, shines upon His own work, excites their holy affections into lively exercise, renders them very efficacious upon their conduct, and thus puts the matters beyond doubt; for while they feel the spirit of dutiful children toward God, they become satisfied concerning His paternal love to them."[15]

The believer should honestly and deliberately compare what he has realized in his personal experience and conduct with the Biblical description of what a Christian should have. When he discovers a close correlation between what the Bible says a Christian should have and what he has recognized in himself, he has evidence of having a sure basis that he is indeed a child of God. That means assurance rests in part on the promises of God and in part on the evidence of the inward grace realized in the experience of the believer. While it is necessary in the beginning to unquestioningly accept the testimony of the Word of God, this additional testimony of the life, comparing favorably with revelation, forms another element in the foundation of assurance.

Assurance Appears in Many Forms

Let us draw near with a true heart in full assurance of faith—Hebrews 10:22a.

That their hearts might be comforted, being knit together in love, and unto all riches of the full assurance of understanding . . .—Colossians 2:2a.

We desire that every one of you do shew the same diligence to the full assurance of hope unto the end—Hebrews 6:11.

The argument for assurance of salvation as presented in the First Epistle of John includes three distinct lines of evidence, one from the Father, one from the Son, and the other from the Holy Spirit. The testimony of the Father runs throughout the argument of the entire epistle although it is sometimes hidden. All who know God from personal communion with Him have positive evidence that He is the most real of all realities. The witness of the Spirit is mentioned again and again and is sometimes mingled with the other lines of evidence. Wesley says that by the testimony of the Spirit he means "inward impressions on the soul, whereby the Spirit of God immediately and directly witnesses to my spirit that I am a child of God, that Jesus Christ hath loved me and given Himself for me, that all my sins are blotted out, and I, even I, am reconciled to God."[16] The incarnate Son, who has made atonement for our sins, rises to testify of the immediate and continuous effect of redemption in each believer. These three lines of evidence, as Keppel says, "are braided together in a three-fold cord which is not easily broken. Indeed, the testimonies are inseparable from that of the Father."[17]

There are three kinds of proof upon which we base our evidence of eternal life; evidence from within, evidence from without, and evidence from above. The evidences we find within are based largely upon the testimony of human consciousness. To give witness to the forgiveness of sins is to speak of a matter with which the individual has had experience. To know that there is no condemnation to them that are in Christ Jesus and to have acted upon that condition in actual confession gives a subjective ground of assurance.

The second source of evidence comes from without and refers primarily to the work of the Holy Spirit in translating inner experience to outward demonstration. When a person realizes that he is walking in newness of life, he has a right to infer from his own conduct that he belongs to the saints of God. A man's judgment upon examining himself and finding that he has the fruit of the Spirit validates his belief in the Word.

The third source of evidence is from God who is above. To be able to say that we know who God is and what He can be to His people is knowledge drawn not from human books but from a divine revelation. In it God gives an account of Himself and illustrates what He has been to the believer. This is not to reason one's self into believing what he would like to feel. The feeling must come from the actual possession and experience. To realize that the Lord has been Shepherd to His own is no vain dream. It is simply a testimony of experience in which the believer finds that what He promised falls in line with what He is performing.

The New Testament speaks of three aspects of assurance: the full assurance of faith (Hebrews 10:22), the full assurance of understanding (Colossians 2:2), and the full assurance of hope (Hebrews 6:11). We refer to the assurance of faith as the discovery of a satisfactory personal relationship with God which is realized through believing in His promise. The consciousness and understanding of our privileges and state in Christ we call the assurance of understanding. The confidence resulting from this discovery of facts may then be called the assurance of hope.

The assurance of faith rests upon the very best evidence that can be found, the eternal Word of the eternal God.[18] Even though our feelings my be changeable and although discouragement may set in, we have in the Word a trustworthy basis for our faith. The person who believes he is saved because God says so is living on the solid rock. The assurance of faith is derived from taking God at His word. This is of utmost importance because it is the germ of all further assurance.

The first act of faith is essential to happy Christian experience but assurance results more from the continued and ever-increasing activity of faith. This growing experience of belief and confidence gradually arises to a clearer consciousness of our position with God. While there are those who hold that "one may go to heaven in a mist, not knowing whither he is going," the assurance of understanding makes possible the knowledge of our present state of our experience with God. It is the privilege of all who receive Christ to have an intellectual as well as an experimental knowledge of Jesus Christ and of our relationship to Him. Paul prayed for the

Colossians that they might have an undimmed confidence of understanding in all the truths that belong to Christian experience. The assurance of understanding is the actual grasping of what God means to those who love Him.

The assurance of hope is an inward witness or testimony of the Holy Spirit who, in addition to giving a comfortable persuasion of our present acceptance with God, gives evidence for a conviction that we will have future and eternal glory. Assurance, therefore, embodies not only a persuasion of our present state of grace, but also a confidence of future salvation. This makes the future of the Christian radiant with the heavenly light of a living hope.

[1] Richard Watson, *Theological Institutes* (New York: Phillips and Hunt, n.d.), Vol. II, p. 271.
[2] T. Austin-Sparks, *God's Spiritual House* (London: Witness and Testimony Publishers, n.d.), p. 24.
[3] L. Berkhof, *The Assurance of Faith* (Grand Rapids, Mich.: Eerdmans), p. 23.
[4] *The Complete Works of Menno Simons* (Elkhart, Ind.: John F. Funk and Brother, 1871), p. 155.
[5] James Hastings, *The Christian Doctrine of Faith* (New York: Scribner's, 1919), p. 295.
[6] Berkhof, op. cit., p. 83.
[7] G. G. Findlay, *The Epistle to the Ephesians* (The Expositor's Bible) (New York: Eaton and Mains, 1905), p. 114.
[8] Hastings, op. cit., p. 296.
[9] Hannah Whitall Smith, *The Open Secret* (New York: Revell, 1885), p. 43.
[10] Findlay, op. cit., p. 114.
[11] Berkhof, op. cit., p. 60.
[12] William Cannon, *The Theology of John Wesley* (New York: Abingdon-Cokesbury, 1946), p. 217.
[13] R. A. Torrey, *What the Bible Teaches* (New York: Fleming H. Revell Co., 1898), p. 481.
[14] Cannon, op. cit., p. 218.
[15] Watson, op. cit., p. 272.
[16] Cannon, op. cit., p. 217.
[17] David Keppel, *That Ye May Know* (New York: Eaton and Mains, 1909), p. 69.
[18] H. S. Miller, *The Christian Worker's Manual* (New York: Doran and Co., 1922), p. 134.

3.

Some People Do Not Have Assurance

A doubleminded man is unstable in all his ways—James 1:8.

The lack of assurance among professing Christians is a disturbing reality. The religious experience of many is entirely inadequate. It may be that the conversion experience was properly motivated and was accompanied with good intentions, but the person failed to grow in the knowledge of God. Frequently such unsatisfactory Christian experience can be traced to inadequate faith. This is the cause of much dissatisfaction and unhappiness. Some people do not have assurance because they have not committed themselves fully to God. Failures of this kind lead to disappointment, false hopes, and sometimes despair.

Inadequate Experience With God Leads to Uncertainty

He that hath the Son hath life; and he that hath not the Son of God hath not life—I John 5:12.

There are some people in the church who profess to be Christians but who are not saved. Such people ought not to have assurance nor indeed can they. If a person wants to know that he is saved, he must first get saved.[1] It is possible for one to be deluded, thinking he is saved when he is not. This may happen to one who has received improper guidance during an attempt at conversion, or it may be due to a failure of actual commitment when seeking God.

Another factor that makes Christian experience inadequate pertains to the matter of pardon. There are people who have sought fellowship with God without confessing their sins. A person who has not dealt satisfactorily with the sin question cannot be redeemed. His sins are not pardoned and he can, therefore, have no genuine peace. He cannot know that he is a child of God, because he is yet in his sins.

Other Christians have no assurance of salvation because of sins of omission in relation to duty toward their fellowmen. In the preceding paragraph we referred to transgressions. We now refer more particularly to failure in carrying out the known will of God. This may express itself in moral issues or in relation to social obligation. For one to be indifferent to the welfare of a neighbor in need is unkind. To be content to let him struggle along without aid is sinful. "Whoso hath this world's good, and seeth his brother have need, and shutteth up his bowels of compassion from him, how dwelleth the love of God in him" (I John 3:17)? Such neglect prohibits assurance.

People who become estranged from their brethren become disinterested in spiritual things. They may even become cynical and bitter in their attitudes, harboring thoughts of hate. They may nurse their injured feelings to a point of resentment, with jealousy and malice filling the heart. People who live in such a state of mind cannot be happy, and their whole spiritual life suffers from social maladjustment. An inadequate personal relationship with God and man forbids assurance.

While it is important that we believe correctly, it is also important that the believer's moral attitude be correct. The conditions for the believer to enjoy the happy experience of assurance are simple but certain. A man must be what his profession requires or he is a hypocrite. Failure to live right destroys the sense of certainty that belongs to the Christian.[2] He must have victory over sin to be assured of salvation.

A child of God must have a godlike nature. To be like God requires more than mere intellectual assent; it requires a change in nature that affects both attitude and conduct. Salvation is introduced by a Gospel of truth and grace, a message that produces moral behavior. It requires the Christian to have an attitude of teachableness, of truth seeking, of honesty, and of right. A Christian profession that lacks in moral control lacks assurance also.

Inadequate Knowledge of God Leads to Mistrust

Whosoever abideth in him sinneth not: whosoever sinneth hath not seen him, neither known him—I John 3:6.

A great deal of the meaning of assurance lies in the knowledge of God's ways of dealing with men. Human nature is inclined to take the keys of the kingdom and forge them into patterns of human design. Instead of meeting the conditions of God's promise of forgiveness, there is a tendency to ignore the need for repentance and to try to develop favor with God by means of good works. This is altogether in vain, for sin requires pardon.

There are many people who rely solely upon their feelings as an evidence of eternal life. This form of inadequacy is a case in which the individual draws from the wrong source for his knowledge of experience. Some people get very happy and feel quite joyful about their experience when they accept Christ. All such must remember that they are not saved because they are happy, but that they are happy because they are saved. There is nothing in the Scripture to indicate that we can know that we are saved because we feel happy. The Bible says persons who believe and trust in the Lord Jesus Christ are saved. It is a knowledge and experience of such truth that gives certitude to Christian faith.

Some people have a wrong evaluation of factors affecting personality. They feel so bad about their experiences and are so sensitive to their many failures and shortcomings that they develop unwholesome feelings of inferiority. Such people usually think they are worthless in the community and useless in the kingdom of God. That sort of attitude is very damaging to assurance. To allow all kinds of accusations from the enemy to lodge in the mind is playing with fire. One must always keep the lines between fact and feeling clearly defined.

The knowledge that produces assurance of salvation is based directly upon the teachings of the Scripture. "Ignorance of the Word of God is one of the greatest sources of the lack of assurance."[3] One who disregards the benefits of Bible reading and neglects his study of the Word will reduce seriously his sense of assurance. A person who is careless about learning to know what the Bible teaches will be indefinite about the requirements of the Christian faith. His experience will rest upon uncertainty and consequently he fails to reach the abundant life.

Knowing what the Scriptures teach about how to get into a good standing with God is the basis for justifying faith. This does not mean that we know we are justified because we are happy. We know that we have a good standing with God upon the basis of having accepted God's plan for reconciling us to Himself. We must believe before we can be justified. The persuasion of our sonship and acceptance with God is based upon a knowledge of our justification. Assurance is therefore one of the results of justification rather than the basis for it. Knowing that we are reinstated in the family of God brings us a sense of satisfaction and certitude both about life and about eternity.

Some people professing Christianity have not related their experience to divine revelation. They have misgivings about God's willingness to forgive. To them forgiveness is a kind of softened disturbance which finds no rest. The fault is a failure to make use of God's promise to forgive. The deceitfulness of human nature, the shallowness of human feelings, and the weakness of human strength are all sources of spiritual defeat. Unless the believer trusts God implicitly, he is certain to have an unsatisfactory Christian experience.

Inadequate Faith in God Fails to Achieve Justification

By grace are ye saved through faith—Ephesians 2:8a.
Ye are risen with him [Christ] through the faith of the operation of God—Colossians 2:12b.

We have already intimated something of the damaging influence of mistrust. "The lack of assurance means the presence of doubt."[4] Of the various kinds of doubt some are related to the personal attitude toward the Gospel while others are related to the state of personal experience. The former is detected by forms of unbelief about the person and teachings of Christ. The latter has less of the rebellious spirit and more indulgence of self-pity; it is usually the result of inadequate experience with God, or of ignorance of the Word of God. In either case, the doubts of a distracted mind and all anxious feelings must be dealt with by a positive trust in God.

There is another form of doubt which is more serious than the doubt of ignorance. The person who has a critical attitude toward divine things and who questions the soundness of Christianity is closing the door to divine blessing. His doubts are more than a lack of assurance; they are actually a form of opposition to faith. We shall deal with this matter again in the following division. At this point we urge the importance of believing wholly what God has said.

Persons who doubt portions of the Word of God are headed for difficulty. To question any single passage that refers directly to the Gospel of Jesus Christ forbids a personal experience of assurance. This is the only message in the world that promises redemption on the basis of experience with God. A person who claims salvation apart from this revelation is simply fooling himself.

Much of this problem results from questionings about the supernatural. The Christian faith and its resulting assurance rest upon belief in the supernatural. Any form of Christian profession which denies the supernatural work of God as revealed in the Scriptures, or as experienced by contemporary Christians, is without the claims of certainty.

The faith that yields assurance of salvation includes two major beliefs. We believe first of all what God says about Jesus Christ; and, secondly, we believe what He says about ourselves. To believe only half of what God says is to rob ourselves of the joy of full assurance. Those who are willing to believe what God says about Christ and who reject what He says about man have only half the truth. Disbelieving what God says about Christ has little more bearing upon Christian assurance than to ignore His revelation about man. The person who denies what God has said about us is in serious spiritual condition.

Inadequate Commitment to God Stunts Spiritual Growth

Ye ought to say, If the Lord will, we shall live, and do this, or that—James 4:15.

There are some people who are very indifferent to spiritual progress in the Christian life. They show little interest in achieving the fuller life in Christ, being very self-satisfied about their own spiritual condition. Such people do not have the deep joy of knowing with certainty their acceptance with God. Many people who fail to grow in their spiritual experience actually turn back. To go on in a life of certitude requires continuous progress in spiritual development.

Some Christians who have encountered difficult circumstances in life have questioned the providence of God. Because they were unable to understand the purpose behind what seemed to them misfortune, they questioned the wisdom of God's dealing. This is essentially a lack of faith. It is a form of hostility which damages assurance of salvation. Such questionings of divine providence do not ordinarily arise when faith is strong and aggressive, or when the life is abounding with good works and actively engaged in Christian service. The following quotation from Berkhof points up very sharply the issues involved in the so-called reverses of life for one who has a dynamic experience with Christ: "They will stand firm in the conviction that a heavenly Father governs their life and all its circumstances, that the trials and adversities that are sent to them are but parental chastisements that minister to their spiritual welfare, that in all their afflictions they enjoy the support of the everlasting arms which will carry them through, and that the light affliction of the present will issue in an eternal weight of glory."[5]

The inference in the preceding paragraph is strong indeed. The person who is consecrated to the will of God and participates wholeheartedly in Christian service has little occasion to be unhappy about his spiritual relationships. Occasionally, however, persons who have followed in the will of God come to a point where consecration fails and they become unwilling to continue to follow. Such disobedience leads to a serious state of doubt and uncertainty. The unhappiness which follows paves the way for satanic questionings which dissipate further the former gleams of assurance.

Some people have missed the blessings of open confession of

Christ. A failure to confess Christ before men can easily lead to questionings of the inner life. People who give no testimony to their own salvation and who fail to witness to the unsaved are inclined to question the reality of their experience. This means that those who are not "all out" for the kingdom of God are subjected to temptations of doubt and uncertainty.

Professed Christians who disobey the known will of God in spite of their attempts at self-justification are unable to convince themselves against the fact of their disobedience. This sets up an inner conflict which disturbs peace of mind and rest of heart. Consequently the blessings of salvation are subjected to the influence of doubt. A person in such a state of mind is soon led to question his own experience with God. Having failed to do what he knows is the will of God and having no inclination to confess his sin and to be reconciled with God leads him away from his assured possession of salvation.

Inadequate Reliance Upon God Creates Spiritual Conflicts

Beloved, if our heart condemn us not, then have we confidence toward God—I John 3:21.

Another hindrance to the experience of assurance is self-reliance. We refer to the attitudes of many sincere people who are relying upon the merits of their own good works to gain favor with God. They feel a sense of duty to do all the good they can in life hoping that the sum of all benevolences and personal deeds will have earned for themselves enough merit to escape hell. Some go so far as to say they do not see how God could ignore justly all the good they have done in the world. Others say they are willing to take chances on the goodness of God to reckon their deeds of sufficient merit to see them through. There are also those who feel they must do all they can to accumulate enough credit toward personal righteousness to appease eventually the wrath of God.

Claims of salvation based upon human merit have a very inadequate basis for assurance. When the amount of deeds rather than the quality of faith is emphasized, a person can never be sure of his score. Whatever hope of being saved such religious philosophy may afford, it has at its best very little current satisfaction. It lays stress upon doing righteousness and pays too little attention to being in Christ. It relies upon human effort and overlooks the importance of divine mercy.

The repudiation of human merit is stated in the words of Paul to Titus, "Not by works of righteousness which we have done, but according to his mercy he saved us, by the washing of regeneration, and renewing of the Holy Ghost" (Titus 3:5). This means that we are not saved in consequence of works even though they were done in righteousness. Man is placed in the state of salvation upon the merits of divine action. We do not effect our salvation by means of self-effort, nor is it a matter of inducing God to favor us in return for human merit. Our redemption is obtained through the offer of divine mercy. Salvation is a gift of grace which we receive through faith.

This principle is stated in the Epistle to the Ephesians also. "For by grace are ye saved through faith; and that not of yourselves: it is the gift of God: Not of works, lest any man should boast" (Ephesians 2:8, 9). The good works which characterize Christians are neither the ground nor the condition of salvation; they are rather the results of God's workmanship. The ground of salvation, as expressed in this passage, is the grace of God; divine grace transcends all human merit. The condition of salvation is faith—faith in the "operation of God" (Colossians 2:12). This is not to be understood as meaning that the believer can generate his own faith unaided by divine grace. The revelation of His Word and the illumination of His Spirit are both essential to faith as the basis upon which it is exercised. Our contention is that the regenerate state is not the result of "unregenerate" works. Salvation is not conveyed to us by effort. It comes through taking God at His Word in Christ.

Any person who seeks salvation through self-effort can never be certain that he is saved. This accounts for much of the uncertainty that exists among professed Christians.

[1] Torrey, op. cit., p. 482.
[2] Hastings, op. cit., p. 271
[3] Torrey, op. cit., p. 483.
[4] Berkhof, op. cit., p. 75.
[5] Berkhof, op. cit., p. 84.

4.

Learn How to Get Assurance

Follow after righteousness, godliness, faith, love, patience, meekness. . . . Lay hold on eternal life, whereunto thou also art called— I Timothy 6:11, 12.

Of the many ordinary means by which assurance can be cultivated we shall consider only a few at this point. In the following paragraphs we will give attention to the place of exercising intellectual belief, to the necessity of heart trust, to the method of appropriating divine grace, to the study of the Word, to prayer, and to Christian graces. Receiving assurance requires a yielding of the will and a decisive commitment. This lays an emphasis upon human responsibility, without ignoring the place of divine grace in the plan of redemption. We are aiming to give practical suggestions to the average Christian with the view to creating better understanding and inspiring more abundant living. These also take us into the realm of daily experience where we find the reality of Christian assurance.

Exercise Belief in the Son of God

*He that believeth on the Son of God hath the witness in himself. . . And this is the record, that God hath given to us eternal life, and this life is in his Son. He that hath the Son hath life—*I John 5:10-12.

It is commonly known among us that there are believers who are weak in faith and distracted by doubts. In some cases these doubts may argue the entire lack of faith. There are specific exhortations in the Scripture which urge such people to examine themselves. Such examination may well start with a careful look at the experience of faith.

Assurance can be cultivated through simply believing God. He says certain things about Himself, certain other things about us, and some other things about the relationship that exists between us. Faith believes what God has said about these things, and assurance follows. Frequently the Scripture has "believing" and "having" joined together. "He that believeth . . . **hath.**"

A person who has a little faith will have only a small measure of assurance. He who believes implicitly enjoys certainty, which finds expression in abundant living and in a joyous hope. As a rule Christians experience a gradual growth of faith. Some people, of course, have violent experiences involving a sudden and tremendous change and a great measure of assurance at once.

It is reasonable to conclude that a person who does not have assurance has not grown sufficiently in his faith. As we have seen in the foregoing division, there are also other factors contributing to a lack of assurance. Our faith may not at first, or at all times, be fully strong. In those cases the persuasion or conviction of religious experience is regulated proportionately.[1] If the faith be at all genuine, God respects the exercise of it, and, though it be weak or strong, encourages growth through His Spirit.

Trust the Promises of God

This is the confidence that we have in him, that, if we ask any thing according to his will, he heareth us—I John 5:14.

Believing refers particularly to the conviction of the truth of the promises of God. Trust belongs to faith but refers more particularly to the sense of confidence. We have "boldness and access with confidence by the faith of him" (Ephesians 3:12). We realize this is a delicate distinction between faith and confidence (trust), but we believe the analysis is justified. It corresponds with John's testimony, "this is the confidence that we have in him" (I John 5:14). The construction of the sentence with the use of the preposition "pros" (in him) is pertinent to our discussion. "It is the strongest preposition that could be used to signify the intimate familiarity of trust."[2] Any lack of trust is indicative of a small measure of faith. A heart that is undivided in its affection, that confides in God as it should, raises the believing soul above the anxieties of life.

"Abraham believed God, and it was counted unto him for righteousness" (Romans 4:3). The meaning of "believed" in the original is more than assent to divine declaration. It indicates that Abraham developed assurance in, and a trustful repose on Jehovah, expecting Him to bring to pass what He promised.[3] His repose was the soul resting not merely on the promises of God but on God Himself. This illustrates the element of assurance that is derived from entire trust in God. We look in the direction of heaven (but not through inward searching) for the basis of our repose. When God can become weary or faint, when He can turn cold toward those whom He has redeemed, then the Christian may find some foundation for fear. Until then we know whom we believe and are satisfied to trust Him. "It is perfectly natural that the trust element in faith should involve a feeling of personal security and safety. To trust is to rely on someone with respect to some vital concern of life. And if this trust be wholehearted and complete, it will banish all fears, set the mind at rest, and fill the heart with a sense of security."[4]

Appropriate the Truth of God

Take heed unto thyself, and unto the doctrine; continue in them: for in doing this thou shalt both save thyself, and them that hear thee—I Timothy 4:16.

Faith produces assurance because it does not stop at the mere acceptance of testimony or declaration. The element of trust takes the soul a step farther and embraces the promise. The next step in this progress of experience is *appropriation,* which is making use of what God offers in daily living. "This means that, where God comes to us in His divine Word with the promise of the forgiveness of sins, of the perfect righteousness in Jesus Christ, and of eternal life in communion with God, we believingly accept the promise and enter into the riches of grace that are freely given us of God, thus becoming 'heirs of God and joint-heirs with Christ.' This assurance consists therefore in a personal appropriation of the general promises of the Gospel."[5]

Promise to the penitent sinner is God's way of proposing to adopt the confessing believer as His own son and to make him heir of everlasting life. When a believing person embraces divine promises using them to satisfy his own conscience, he believes in their reality for the present and in their soundness for the future. Such assurance is based directly on the Word of God. It also rests upon the believer's acceptance of the promises the Word contains.

The Holy Spirit increases faith by enabling the believer to continuously appropriate the promises of God. Just as one grows in grace, he grows also in the experience of appropriation and consequently has an increased measure of assurance. This means that the Christian enters into a life of certainty and that this certainty increases as the believer continues his appropriation of grace.

The Christian can say with the Apostle Paul, "We are of the truth." To bring this truth into personal experience and to translate it into life is to say, "We know that God dwells in us." This goes far beyond the boundary of intellectual assertion; it is a claim of experience. The intellectual conviction has been supported by personal appropriation. That is how the experience of God and man meet; it is where the divine and human make acquaintance; it is the case of Creator and the person formed holding communion. When God finds man in a receptive mood, and man knows God in terms of experience, man is said to have appropriated the truth of God.

Study the Word of God

Study to shew thyself approved unto God, a workman that needeth not to be ashamed, rightly dividing the word of truth— II Timothy 2:15.

The three elements of inner response to the promises of God are belief, trust, and appropriation. The basis of these elements is divine revelation. Therefore, in order to make progress in the experience of assurance we must diligently study the Bible. One who is searching for certainty should give particular attention to the glorious promise of forgiveness. He should search for specific statements that relate to the plan of salvation. This forms an outward basis for assurance.

Assurance must rest upon something more permanent than our own states of feeling. Everybody knows very well that emotions vary a great deal according to circumstances. Assurance of salvation does not waver with the changing states of feeling. Assurance that rests upon the unchanging Word remains steadfast.

All of us know the experience of being "turned around" in a strange environment. The writer was traveling at night, going south by train. Upon waking in the morning, he looked out of the window and had a feeling of going north. He knew that he should be traveling in the opposite direction from that which his feelings were indicating. With all the repeated effort to conquer those feelings, to turn himself right, there was no change in the sense of direction. Finally he resorted to the timetable and checked the schedule of the train on which he was traveling. He checked carefully from one small station to the next and ascertained from the names of stations in their order that he was actually traveling south, the direction in which he ought to go. Without any further attempt to force himself to feel that he was going south, he had no difficulty believing with certainty that he was on the way to his destination. So it is with the Word of God, which charts the direction in which a man goes. One can make observations in his own experience, checking them against the Word, and know the direction in which he is going. Some of these tests are presented in Chapters 7 and 8.

Pray for the Wisdom of God

The wisdom that is from above is first pure, then peaceable, gentle, and easy to be intreated, full of mercy and good fruits . . .
—James 3:17.

The study of the Word is greatly improved by the experience of prayer. In prayer one makes application of the promises he has read in the Scriptures. It is the human response in communion with God. To learn the deep lessons of spiritual communication is to increase confidence in spiritual reality. It gives to the believer a sense of connection with divine power and grace. Receiving answers to prayer deepens the sense of the divine Presence.

It becomes more and more clear to the growing Christian that the Word of God invites the saint to make requests. Through simple, childlike trust, the believer can approach God and ask Him for assurance. It will not come in any form of magic, but it will come in response to prayer requests. James said, "Let him ask of God." This has its application in the realm of Christian assurance. It needs to be an honest request in which one yields himself to the will of God. The element of decision in yielding self to God secures divine approval and reduces any sense of uncertainty in spiritual relationships.

Prayer becomes a vital factor also in making use of blessing received through the ordinances. Christ established the ordinances to provide objective symbols of inner experience. In themselves they do not produce assurance, but they serve as a channel through which God reassures the soul. This, of course, presupposes that the believer brings an experience of salvation into his observance. To appropriate these blessings requires a deep sense of communion, for God expresses Himself through the silent and sacred symbols only when the participating soul is having prayer experience. In that way these external observances increase assurance. To a trustful soul participating in an ordinance, God gives the reassurance of having the common salvation.

Cultivate Christian Graces

Be thou an example of the believers, in word, in conversation, in charity, in spirit, in faith, in purity—I Timothy 4:12.

We do not find our assurance in the lives of other Christians. The marks of true faith originate within the Christian himself. They agree with the standards of a holy life as described in the Word of God. One has assurance when he is sure that he loves God and has a holy desire to do God's will. When he has sorrow on account of sin and a longing for holiness, when he experiences hatred of sinful deeds and a resistance to the forces of evil, he knows his experience is in accord with what the Bible says about genuine Christian experience. "The clearer these Christian graces shine forth and the more abundant they are, the greater will be the measure of assurance which they engender."[6]

Peter gives a strong exhortation to his readers to make their calling and election sure by cultivating a Christian disposition. Having faith as the root of experience, they should proceed to virtuous living. He is calling for a life that impresses the observer with its consistency in the light of the requirements of righteousness. He names as examples such graces as temperance, patience, godliness, and brotherly love. II Peter 1:5-7. This clearly indicates that one may increase his sense of assurance by increasing the virtues which are a part of Christian experience. As one reflects on the Christian graces in his own life, he is basing his assurance on a comparison of experience with the statement of revelation. When the two agree, it gives to the Christian a sense of certainty about the reality of his own experience.

Assurance is the fruit of honest reflection upon the existing state of salvation. We must give to ourselves an intelligent account of Christian evidences. With the use of analysis and comparison, we obtain a reasonable insight into our state of grace. This can be done with any area of experience in which disturbing questions may arise. The persuasion of the reality of faith and the conviction of a satisfactory standing with God are convincing evidences of eternal life. As a rule, doubts do not arise where there is a strong and active faith.

When a believer is conscious of having power over sin, he is encouraged to resist temptation. When he realizes this power within himself, he finds it easier to break off the tendencies toward evil. When he finds that he has grace to conquer evil desires and passion, he is made more courageous in his conflict with sin. The possession of such moral courage confirms his relation to God. Power to overcome evil gives a sense of deep desire for a manner of conduct which his moral sense approves. This builds up childlike confidence in God. The Christian knows by experience that he is in vital connection with the source of righteousness.

Man has an inner faculty with which to search and judge his own actions and motives. When such searching yields a report of a satisfactory state, it bears witness to holiness. The inner assurance is always connected with the external. Having the fruits of holiness or the testimony of a conscience void of offense toward God gives a sense of certainty about spiritual experience. This is within the range of normal experience in the life of every Christian. When the believer looks at his own faith and his spiritual condition in this way he can determine the genuineness of his faith, the health of his spiritual state, the certainty of his sonship, and the soundness of his claim to the eternal inheritance. These things, explicitly stated in the Word of God, are elements of assurance which can be obtained by reflection. It must be remembered, however, that we do not gain this assurance by reflection alone. "Whatever assurance may be attained in this way, can only result from a true spiritual insight into the promises of God; from a self-examination that is performed with candid honesty, with great thoroughness, in a prayerful frame of mind, and above all under the illuminating influence of the Holy Spirit; and from a conclusion that is based on a correct interpretation of the promises of God, and of such Christian graces as are clearly and unmistakably recognized as fruit of the Spirit."[7]

---

[1] Watson, op. cit., p. 271.
[2] William Pope, *A Compendium of Christian Theology* (Cleveland, Thomas and Mattill, n.d.), Vol. III, p. 119.
[3] Berkhof, op. cit., p. 38.
[4] Ibid., p. 40.
[5] Ibid., p. 35.
[6] Ibid., p. 79.
[7] Ibid., p. 68.

5.

Assurance Relies on Essential Christian Experience

These things have I written unto you that believe on the name of the Son of God; that ye may know that ye have eternal life, and that ye may believe on the name of the Son of God—I John 5:13.

A child of God accepts Jesus Christ and pledges allegiance to Him and His Word. So far as he knows himself he is conformed to the will of God. He has a witness within himself that he is right with God. He has met the conditions for salvation. But there is yet a greater witness to testify to the position he now has in Christ Jesus. The Word says, "He that believeth on the Son hath everlasting life." "He that hath the Son hath life." These things have been written as a testimony to help him know that he has eternal life.

To know that one has eternal life is knowledge essential to happiness. The First Epistle of John was written to deepen the sense of security in the hearts of Christian people. It informs the redeemed on points of spiritual experience relating to inward peace and to a firm confidence toward God. While there may be a few people who have eternal life and do not know it, that is not a normal Christian experience. People who are not sure of their salvation, who entertain doubts and misgivings, or who do not realize their possessions and privileges in Christ, are lacking in essential knowledge. It is our purpose in this division to point out the kind of information that will lay the foundation for assurance of eternal life.

Forgiveness From God Is Assured to Believers

And you, being dead in your sins and the uncircumcision of your flesh, hath he quickened together with him [Christ], having forgiven you all trespasses—Colossians 2:13.

Here is the statement of an all-embracing pardon, "having forgiven you all trespasses." This is a condition that obtains by the very nature of the new life; that is to say, the new life from the risen Lord implies forgiveness. It comes from the work of regeneration. People who were doomed to die have received pardon; this illustrates for us eternal life. To know that our sins are forgiven is evidence that we have been born again. This means literally that God has bestowed His favor upon us, and that we know it.

The knowledge of forgiveness of sins is based upon the promises of God. All who seek Him and call upon Him, forsaking their ways and their evil thoughts, have the promise of forgiveness. "Let the wicked forsake his way, and the unrighteous man his thoughts: and let him return unto the Lord, and he will have mercy upon him; and to our God, for he will abundantly pardon" (Isaiah 55:7). We need no further evidence; this is proof enough of acquittal. God's justice has been satisfied with the sin offering, and now He is ready to release the judgment against sin for all who meet the conditions that qualify for pardon. We believe His Word and act accordingly.

For God sent not his Son into the world to condemn the world; but that the world through him might be saved. He that believeth on him is not condemned: but he that believeth not is condemned already, because he hath not believed in the name of the only begotten Son of God—John 3:17, 18.

The believer is not condemned; there is no sentence against him. God has received Christ's sacrifice as the atonement for sins, and has lifted the judgment against all who accept the provision secured by Christ's death. "Through this man [Christ] is preached unto you the forgiveness of sins: And by him all that believe are justified from all things" (Acts 13:38, 39a). There is no "hangover" in this. The penitent sinner who believes in Christ is given a new standing with God. That means Christ secures for him forgiveness, remission of sins. The condemnation that was upon him is dissolved; God holds nothing against him.

He that heareth my word, and believeth on him that sent me, hath everlasting life, and shall not come into condemnation; but is passed from death unto life—John 5:24.

This passage emphasizes two conditions upon which we receive eternal life. He that obeys the sayings of Christ and trusts in God shall not come into judgment. On the contrary, however, he that rejects Christ, and does not receive His words, "hath one that judgeth him: the word that I have spoken, the same shall judge him in the last day" (John 12:48). The positive statement of this verse emphasizes the need of accepting the Word of God as a rule for life, as much as accepting Jesus Christ as a substitute in atonement. It is clear, however, that one who meets these conditions is neither under condemnation with the world now, nor shall he come into judgment in the age to come. The acquittal makes real both our present standing with God and our prospects for the future. Such knowledge is beyond human reason, but it is just as real and easy to receive as the deductions of natural reasoning.

*Ye were without Christ, being aliens from the commonwealth of Israel, and strangers from the covenants of promise, having no hope, and without God in the world: But now in Christ Jesus ye who sometimes were far off are made nigh by the blood of Christ—*Ephesians 2:12, 13.

Salvation is infinitely more than cold and formal reception into the royal courts of a great Sovereign. God invites us into His intimate presence; He wants us to be near Him. Having become united with Christ, we are living in a precious nearness to God. Christ brought us within the range of His saving grace and redemptive power.

The word "now" is an emphatic form, meaning "this very moment."[1] It refers to the present experience as a result of being made (created or regenerated) nigh to God. On the merits of Christ's blood we are invited to come into the holy presence of God to delight in His glory. The regenerating work of the Spirit actually puts us near to the Father. A personal knowledge of this position gives the believer a blessed assurance of divine blessing.

Acceptance by God Is a Present Reality

*Having predestinated us unto the adoption of children by Jesus Christ to himself, according to the good pleasure of his will, to the praise of the glory of his grace, wherein he hath made us accepted in the beloved—*Ephesians 1:5, 6.

The Father and the Son in their blessed fellowship with each other have chosen to make the sonship of Christ become ours, too. Of course, the eternal relationship between Christ and God cannot be made ours, but in Christ we share the blessedness, the security, and the honor of that relationship.[2] We have the same kind of life, having access to the eternal fountains of the life of God.

The word *accepted* must be understood in terms of divine grace. His favors are graciously bestowed upon us for His own pleasure and glory. He makes us one with Christ in order to give us a real part in our Lord's own welcome to the Father. This is very significant when we understand the natural disobedience and rebellion of the human heart. We were helplessly and hopelessly alienated from God. Christ stepped in between us and God and through the redeeming power of His blood lifted us to a position where we could regain the favor of God. Now, in Christ, God has freely bestowed upon us the glory of His grace and has given us a welcome to His own heart.

Adoption by God Confirms Filial Relationship

Behold, what manner of love the Father hath bestowed upon us, that we should be called the sons of God: therefore the world knoweth us not, because it knew him not. Beloved, now are we the sons of God—I John 3:1, 2a.

This relationship of children to the Father is the result of God's great love to men. He gave His Son that we should not perish. In obtaining everlasting life as a present reality, we are able to rejoice in Him with "joy unspeakable and full of glory." The ground of our assurance lies in the consciousness of our filial relationship.[3] This is a great source of Christian happiness and courage. Death and judgment need not cause us to falter or fear. The eternal issues of destiny do not disturb us. We know where we belong and on whom we are counting for an entrance into the happy eternal realm.

This does not lay the burden of proof upon the final issue. We do not wait until Jesus comes to find out whether or not we are the sons of God. That is determined by other means here and now. In human relationships a son needs no unconditional guarantee that he will receive a full portion of his father's inheritance to convince him of his present position as a son in the family of his father. While we recognize that our continuance in the family of God is conditional upon our faithfully abiding in Him, this condition does not in the least hinder our present assurance of sonship. "**Now** are **we** the sons of God."

But when the fulness of the time was come, God sent forth his Son, made of a woman, made under the law, to redeem them that were under the law, that we might receive the adoption of sons. And because ye are sons, God hath sent forth the Spirit of his Son into your hearts, crying, Abba, Father—Galatians 4:4-6.

Christ's incarnation and suffering qualified Him to become the satisfactory sin offering. It is through His death that we are acquitted. Adoption into the family of God is dependent upon the pardon we receive. When we receive forgiveness, the Spirit is sent into our hearts to establish divine fellowship. This is God's witness and testimony that we are His children.

The Son was sent, that through His death and intercession we might receive this royal adoption. The Spirit of His Son was sent to assure us of our sonship and of the filial relationships which that position in the royal family implies. Just as the purpose of His Son has been actually accomplished at Calvary, so the purpose of the Spirit is now realized in our lives. He makes us conscious of being the legal joint heirs with Christ in the eternal kingdom. He gives us the right and inclination to address God as "Our Father."

But as many as received him [Christ], to them gave he power to become the sons of God, even to them that believe on his name— John 1:12.

This passage refers to our privileges in Christ as members of the household of God. Having received Jesus Christ as our Substitute, as our Saviour, and as our Lord, we are given the right to be the children of God.

*If thou shalt confess with thy mouth the Lord Jesus, and shalt believe in thine heart that God hath rasied him from the dead, thou shalt be saved. For with the heart man believeth unto righteousness; and with the mouth confession is made unto salvation—*Romans 10:9, 10.

By the exercise of a genuine faith in Christ and a full confession of Christ as Saviour and Lord, we secure salvation. That means we belong to the family of God; this is occasion for great rejoicing. We are partakers of the greatest possible honor—the honor of divine royalty. We are in prospect of the greatest possible heritage—the eternal kingdom. We are in possession of the greatest possible existence—partakers of eternal life.

*Wherefore the law was our schoolmaster to bring us unto Christ, that we might be justified by faith. But after that faith is come, we are no longer under a schoolmaster. For ye are all the children of God by faith in Christ Jesus—*Galatians 3:24-26.

The law was intended to teach lessons of God's justice and holiness as well as the fact of man's depravity. It prepared man for the understanding of the office and work of Christ. While the saints under the old dispensation were saved by faith, they were limited in the matter of their assurance. It was necessary for them to make atonement for their sins at least once every year. Now we are no longer held back from the free exercise of faith, for trusting in Christ makes us sons. We are sons by faith and enjoy the privileges of resident sonship.

The Position in Christ Qualifies for Divine Blessings

*Giving thanks unto the Father, which hath made us meet to be partakers of the inheritance of the saints in light: Who hath delivered us from the power of darkness, and hath translated us into the kingdom of his dear Son—*Colossians 1:12, 13.

God in His infinite love and in the sacrifice of His Son has made us fit to share in the divine inheritance. We were once children of disobedience, walking according to the fashion of this world, in submission to the power of Satan. But through our acceptance of Jesus Christ and in our coming to God, we were delivered from evil and have been transferred to another kingdom. We have been translated into the kingdom of Christ. He paid the ransom price for our redemption and through His resurrection has made victorious living possible.

The call to thanksgiving arises from the things God has done for Christians. This passage is dealing with completed action. The inheritance to which we have fallen heir seems "to include the whole portion of spiritual blessings allotted to the human family of God."[4] In order to bring the believer into possession of these blessings, God has transferred him out from under the rule of darkness into the realm where Christ rules. This kingdom will have its full realization in the future, but the saints are registered in it now. The enrollment brings with it at once the foretaste of eternal blessedness.

*There is therefore now no condemnation to them which are in Christ Jesus, who walk not after the flesh, but after the Spirit—*Romans 8:1.

Noah and his family were in the great ark at the time of the flood; because of their position in the ark they were safe from the judgment of God. On the night of their departure from Egypt the children of Israel in their blood-sprinkled houses were safe from the plague of the Destroyer. Rahab was safe from the destruction of the Israelites because she was abiding in a house which had a scarlet thread hanging from its window. So the Christian who is in Christ Jesus is free from condemnation. He has no occasion to be uneasy about his past sins, for atonement has been made for them. One who is in Christ Jesus—who has his heart sprinkled with the blood of Jesus Christ and does not walk after the flesh—feels no sense of condemnation, because he knows God has accepted our Saviour's sacrifice for his sins.

This simple phrase "in Christ Jesus" has deep spiritual implications and has far-reaching effects in its application to the believer's life. Our union with Christ has deep meaning in its relation to assurance. It points directly to the heart of Christian experience. It refers to the most essential factor in the believer's present state of grace. To understand our position "in Christ" is to know the sphere and the supernaturalness of Christian living.

The Possessions in Christ Are Gifts of Divine Grace

*Therefore being justified by faith, we have peace with God through our Lord Jesus Christ—*Romans 5:1.

Knowing that God is satisfied with the sin offering which was sacrificed on Calvary, we are at ease and have a peace which surpasses understanding. God's wrath against us has been removed, for we have come from a state of condemnation into justification. God's justice has been satisfied in the substitutionary death of Christ. When we exercise faith in Him as our Saviour, it results in the removal of the curse of the Mosaic Law and of the wrath of God. God therefore reckons us acquitted—righteous. Knowing that this transaction has been completed gives peace and joy.

The many possessions we acquire through Christ cannot be enumerated here. We have chosen "peace" as a good example of what God gives in response to the exercise of the believer's faith and obedience. The certitude and the present tense of this verse is characteristic of the language in the New Testament: "we **have** peace," "we **have** access," "we **have** hope," "we **have** redemption," etc. If we have anything that pertains to salvation, we have these possessions as a personal and present asset.

Now we have received, not the spirit of the world, but the spirit which is of God; that we might know the things that are freely given to us of God—I Corinthians 2:12.

It is God's purpose that the redeemed should "know the things that are freely given to us." The Holy Spirit resides in the believer to give him a consciousness of these divine blessings. They are gifts of free grace and include all the kingdom blessings. In a normal Christian life there is a growing discernment of these things. The believer becomes more and more conscious of his own state of grace and acquires personal knowledge through the Spirit. As his faith ripens, as his experience broadens, as his love increases, and as his devotion deepens, the Spirit gives a profound sense of gratitude and security. He gives rest and satisfaction to the soul.[5]

The Privileges in Christ Come Through Divine Mediation

My little children, these things write I unto you, that ye sin not. And if any man sin, we have an advocate with the Father, Jesus Christ the righteous: And he is the propitiation for our sins: and not for ours only, but also for the sins of the whole world—I John 2:1,2.

One of the greatest secrets of happiness and assurance in Christian living is to know what to do with sin. None can say that he has not sinned, nor that he has no sin. It is understood, however, that having been forgiven and cleansed by the blood, the Christian does not need to sin. "If any man sin," that is, in case one who has tasted forgiveness and eternal life should commit sin, there is provision made for his restoration. "We have an advocate with the Father"; He is One whose intercession avails in cases of emergency.

It is a normal condition for a person who "walks in the light" to live victoriously. Nevertheless, even to such a one sin is not impossible. If he should be so unfortunate as to fall into sin, he need not give up his confidence in God, as though that one sin made void his entire experience of eternal life. Provision is made to be restored from such a lapse. "We have an advocate with the Father," One toward whom the Father is graciously disposed.

We must not forget that sin in the life of the believer is a contradiction. That is, the practice of sin is altogether contrary to the Christian pattern. Scripture relating to sin, as found in I John 3:8, 9, uses the verb in the present tense of the Greek and denotes continued or habitual action. The verb in the passage quoted at the head of this division is in the subjunctive aorist tense and therefore refers to a single occurrence. It is this kind of sin for which there is an Advocate with the Father. There is no indication that God grants reconciliation to the persistent wrongdoer. Penitence and confession qualify one to engage the Lawyer to plead his case. "If we confess" is the keynote both to the effectiveness of the Advocate and to the qualification for forgiveness from the righteous Judge.[6]

The Christian lives in an experience of perpetual pardon, a pardon not to be obtained on the mere asking. For that reason we must read on: "He is the propitiation for our sins." This leaves no room for men to hold a light and easy notion about sin. The priest who approaches God on behalf of the guilty must have something to offer (Hebrews 8:3). The pleader cannot get into court without a propitiation. He must have something with which to satisfy the offended holiness of God. There must be some guarantee that the offense shall cease. The Advocate must take something with Him or His plea will have no avail. This propitiation for our sins was supplied altogether by Jesus. There was no ground in humanity, outside of Him, upon which any intercessor could make an acceptable plea. So He presented Himself. "**He** is the propitiation" (I John 2:2).

There is also a condition required of the believer. Only the penitent one, the one confessing his sins and believing in the merits of Christ's death, can claim the right to forgiveness. This suffices because there is virtue in relying upon the expiation made by "the blood of Jesus."

It is very assuring to the believer to know that the Father is not hard to persuade. He is not inclined to raise occasions against the believer nor does He press the claims of the law to his disfavor. He has before God a righteous Advocate, justice pleading with love for man's release. The character of the "lawyer" is above reproach. His name and record guarantee an audience with the Judge. The One who pleads the case is qualified with human affinity and a divine prerogative, with merit and power that are essential to the case. Since it is Jesus Christ who speaks for man, He being all that the Gospel records of Him and being all that His apostles knew Him to be, we may trust completely in His intercessions.[7] We are assured of His ability to handle the case. The sinless One is pleading for the guilty; He has a right to approach the Judge. The righteous One is pleading for the unrighteous; He has fulfilled the conditions of the law. He will urge no argument and take no position in our case that does not gain the approval of a compassionate Father.

"The Advocate throws His life into the plea; He speaks by His blood. He steps, as one would say, from the pleaders' bench into the dock to cover the prisoner's person with His own. He puts His unspotted holiness and the wealth of His being at the service and in the place of the criminal . . . in such form as is possible and fitting to innocence, [that] He may save him from its [sin's] fatal issue and recover him for goodness and for God."[8]

We see then how Christ is well qualified to speak for us. His accomplished work, His divine person, and His present activities all unite to make our standing with God an acceptable position. Although sin breaks fellowship with God, the confession of that sin allows the faithful and just God to forgive and restore the penitent child. The Christian gets an audience with God for such an occasion because of the value of Christ's atonement. Christ is certain to secure our pardon, for He is righteous and pleads our cause on the merits of His own shed blood and in response to our personal faith in Him.

---

[1] H. S. Miller, *The Book of Ephesians* (Harrisburg, Pa.: The Evangelical Press, 1931), p. 90.

[2] R. W. Dale, *The Epistle to the Ephesians* (New York: George H. Doran Company), p. 44.

[3] George Findlay, *Fellowship in the Life Eternal* (London: Hodder and Stoughton, 1849), p. 236.

[4] Joseph A. Beet, *Commentary on Colossians* (London: Hodder and Stoughton, 1890), p. 141.

[5] Findlay, op. cit., p. 139.

[6] Ibid., p. 114.

[7] Ibid., p. 117.

[8] Ibid., p. 129.

6.

Assurance Involves Essential Biblical Knowledge

The Right to Our Inheritance Is Certain

For if ye live after the flesh, ye shall die: but if ye through the Spirit do mortify the deeds of the body, ye shall live. For as many as are led by the Spirit of God, they are the sons of God. For ye have not received the spirit of bondage again to fear; but ye have received the Spirit of adoption, whereby we cry, Abba, Father. The Spirit itself beareth witness with our spirit, that we are the children of God—Romans 8:13-16.

The context preceding this passage makes it clear that "if any man have not the Spirit of Christ, he is none of his." It is also clear that a person who is led by the Spirit is certainly a child of God. There is a threefold witness within the believer: one is the result of reflection upon experience of being led by the Spirit, another is the direct testimony of the Spirit to the soul by an inward impression, and the third is an indirect testimony of the Spirit's agreement with our spirit. In these three lines of evidence we find the basis of confidence in our filial relationship with God. To know that we are sons of God is to be assured of our right to His inheritance.

The testimony that comes of experience in being led by the Spirit is derived from observation of circumstances and personal reaction. It is really the testimony of our own spirit. This is inferred from the statement of Paul when he mentions a joint witness to our salvation. The Holy Spirit gives a testimony concurrently with the testimony of our own spirit.[1] This means the partner to the Holy Spirit is our own spirit.[2] The assertions of verse 16 are clearly dependent upon verse 14. Only those who know God's leading as a personal experience can have a testimony in joint witness with the Holy Spirit.[3] Man's own spirit is recognized in verse 15. The familiar address, "we cry, Abba, Father," is a testimony which reflects the speaker's consciousness of a filial relationship with God. This "cry" of intimacy is not the voice of man's lower human nature; it is the expression of his spirit, the highest level of experience and the nearest to God. Even this is prompted and tempered by the Spirit *in whom* we cry, "Abba, Father." This affords proof that we are the children of God. It inspires in us childlike confidence with which we address Him in terms of filial intimacy and with which we sense our right to all the allotments (inheritance) of His kingdom blessings.

A second line of evidence is the testimony of the Holy Spirit to the spirit of the believer. Berkhof quotes Wesley as saying, "By the testimony of the Spirit, I mean an inward impression on the soul, whereby the Spirit of God immediately and directly witnesses to my spirit that I am a child of God, that Jesus Christ hath loved me and given Himself for me, that all my sins are blotted out, and I, even I, am reconciled to God."[4] The Spirit functions in the inner man and impresses upon the believer the special and loving care of the Father. He is the medium through whom we have free access to the Father, who gives us the title to the heavenly inheritance.

The third testimony is the Holy Spirit's joint witness along with our spirit. We are born of the Spirit and He will not leave the voice of the believer to stand alone. It is a blessed reassurance to have the mighty testimony of the Holy Spirit borne along with the feeble voice of our own spirit. He unites His witness with ours to give us complete certainty. We often receive human testimony not half as well authenticated. Shall we doubt the witness of the God of truth and make Him a lair? God has borne witness concerning His Son, that every one who believes in Him has life. The believer has the witness in his own spirit, but here is the added testimony of the Holy Spirit.

The right to all the blessings of the kingdom rests upon the acceptance of the provision for redemption and the human appropriation of divine grace. The evidence that Christians are heirs of eternal glory is cumulative. In addition to the three lines of evidence submitted above in relation to experience with the Holy Ghost, we have further testimony from the faithfulness of God. Not only do the objective promises give us hope but we also receive confidence from the fact that God is trustworthy. Certitude rests primarily upon the object of faith. It is not enough to be conscious of having the indwelling Spirit, or of having a satisfactory moral condition for judgment. We need an intimate confidence in God, a sense of present sonship in the family of God.

The Earnest of Our Inheritance Is Given

And grieve not the holy Spirit of God, whereby ye are [were,

RSV] sealed unto the day of redemption—Ephesians 4:30.

Now he which stablisheth us with you in Christ, and hath anointed us, is God; who hath also sealed us, and given the earnest of the Spirit in our hearts—II Corinthians 1:21, 22.

The seal is a mark of ownership. Paul's audience was well acquainted with the practice of making an impression in soft clay with an engraving of the owner's likeness to give an article the stamp of ownership. The seal was also used to show the genuineness of official statements and to guard against injury to property, or to protect against theft. It served as an instrument of official protection, approval, and ownership.[5] Here the figure is used to indicate the spiritual mark God places upon His child.

In the Old Testament the mark of circumcision was used to identify the people of God. In this dispensation the Holy Spirit is performing a similar but more real spiritual function. The stamp of God upon us is the indwelling presence of the Holy Spirit. As is indicated in Ephesians 1:13, those who believe in Christ and are united with Him have met the condition that qualifies a person for the affixing of the seal of God upon the heart. The sealing takes place in virtue of being united with Christ. Receiving the seal—the gift of the Holy Spirit—proves that God is ready to share with the believer the blessings procured by Christ.

It is important for the Christian to observe that having become a believer *ye were sealed.* This refers to the time of regeneration, when the Spirit effected a new birth. He came into the heart to dwell in constant fellowship with the believers.

The present aspect of this experience is extended to the future. The seal is given in view of the day of redemption, when God shall claim the property He has purchased. We are sealed because of the work of Christ. The value of His atonement is realized now, but its worth to the soul will become fully known in the day of final redemption.

The Corinthian passage indicates another aspect of this figure. The seal has yet another use; it is a symbol of assurance.[6] The Holy Spirit makes an impression upon the soul. When His presence becomes evident by an inner change of desire and dynamic, and when the subsequent virtues are manifested outwardly, the testimony is convincing. The witness we have within is not only the testimony of our own consciousness but also of His attestation.

In whom ye also trusted, after that ye heard the word of truth, the gospel of your salvation: in whom also after that ye believed, ye were sealed with that holy Spirit of promise, which is the earnest of our inheritance until the redemption of the purchased possession, unto the praise of his glory—Ephesians 1:13, 14.

Now he that hath wrought us for the selfsame thing is God, who also hath given unto us the earnest of the Spirit—II Corinthians 5:5.

The same Spirit who is impressed upon us, marking us as God's purchased possession, is also referred to as "an earnest" of the inheritance which is to be ours. An earnest is a part payment of the thing to be possessed, given at the time of purchase in assurance that the full payment will follow at the time of complete possession.

In the new birth the Spirit regenerates and marks the believer with the stamp of eternal life. In addition, He is the earnest of a Spirit-filled life and, in filling the life, becomes the earnest of coming blessing and glory.[7] The Spirit's presence in us is therefore an evidence that we will come into possession of our eternal inheritance.

The Spirit is a foretaste of the joys and delights of heaven. Observe the love of God He sheds abroad in our hearts (Romans 5:5), the transfiguration He performs in us (II Corinthians 3:18), the manifestations of divine virtue (Galatians 2:22, 23), and the fellowship He sustains; they are all the kind of experience heaven will afford. Life in the Spirit is like the marvelous Eshcol grapes the two spies brought from Canaan to Israel in the wilderness. The two whose faithfulness accompanied their token of the plentiful land eventually came into full possession of their inheritance. The Spirit is a token of what heaven contains. There can be no doubt of its reality and blessedness. God has given the evidence and more; He has given a share of His promise in advance of the final distribution. The earnest we have is not only a part payment of future inheritance, but it is a fair sample of the glory it contains. The "full payment" will be of the same character as that which we now possess in the earnest.

For we know that the whole creation groaneth and travaileth in pain together until now. And not only they, but ourselves also, which have the firstfruits of the Spirit, even we ourselves groan within ourselves, waiting for the adoption, to wit, the redemption of our body—Romans 8:22, 23.

This present witness of the Holy Spirit in our lives is the "firstfruits" of the Spirit. All who have the witness of the Spirit within are, therefore, waiting for the full inheritance that shall accompany the return of our Lord. Before we receive that inheritance, there must be a redemption of the body. When He comes, He will change our vile bodies that they might be fashioned "like unto his glorious body" (Philippians 3:21). With the present assurance of sonship and the living hope in Christ's return, "we know that . . . we shall be like him; for we shall see him as he is" (I John 3:2).

The redeemed are still living in a sinful world exposed to the seductions of evil and hostile forces. We are waiting for the final measure of redemption. We look for the time when our ranson shall receive its full return of glory. We hope for the day of eternal triumph, the day of the perfection of our salvation. Until then we have the "firstfruits"—the blessings of the Spirit—to reassure our hearts of complete and final redemption.

The Hope of Our Inheritance Is in Effect

Blessed be the God and Father of our Lord Jesus Christ, which according to his abundant mercy hath begotten us again unto a lively hope by the resurrection of Jesus Christ from the dead, to an inheritance incorruptible, and undefiled, and that fadeth not away, reserved in heaven for you, who are kept by the power of God through faith unto salvation ready to be revealed in the last time—
I Peter 1:3-5.

The change which is effected by the regenerative work of the Holy Spirit at the time of conversion is not only a change of nature and a change of position with God, but it also includes a change of outlook. When God performed "His workmanship" of this new creation by Christ Jesus, He gave us the birth of a living hope. Christ was the "firstfruits" from among the dead, and therefore we know that He has had victory over the power of death. The new creation in Christ Jesus brings us into a vital relationship with God and yields a living hope. It points to the time when we shall enjoy the incorruptible inheritance reserved in heaven for us. Knowing that the promises of God are sure, we look for the return of His Son and for His glory.

We are saved by hope, the element of expectancy in faith. We hope for things unseen and realize a present sense of reality in them. We see the future possession of them as within our reach and trust God to fulfill His promise. Confidence in the character of God to perform His Word and a persuasion that His promises are made to us personally, give assurance of eventual possession of the things for which we hope.

*Let not your heart be troubled: ye believe in God, believe also in me. In my Father's house are many mansions: if it were not so, I would have told you. I go to prepare a place for you. And if I go and prepare a place for you, I will come again, and receive you unto myself; that where I am, there ye may be also—*John 14:1-3.

There are many hearts troubled with spiritual doubts today, as there were when Jesus gave His disciples this word of cheer and comfort. There is really no occasion, however, for Christians to become dismayed about prevailing circumstances, because our trust in God and our belief in His Son give a hopeful outlook on life and hold bright prospects for eternity. In the "Father's house" are many mansions. God has made abundant provision for a blessed eternity of fellowship with Him. In the meantime, He invites the redeemed to anticipate this entrance into the glories of His abode. The spiritual fellowship we have with the Son and with the Spirit here is only a foretaste of what the future holds. It will have its consummation in endless reunion and in eternal fellowship with the saints and with the royal Godhead in the "Father's house." Christ has gone to prepare the place and expects us to be with Him where He is.

To believe in God is to confide in His love. Though we witness the crash of world empires, although the earth should tremble beneath our feet, and even though heaven and earth should pass away, we have a sure refuge in Him. Our hope is an anchor that rests securely in Christ at the throne of God.

Christ will not always be hidden from the view of men on earth as He now is. He will someday be fully revealed so that "every eye shall see him"; when He appears, the saints shall be manifested with Him in His great glory. "When Christ, who is our life, shall appear, then shall ye also appear with him in glory" (Colossians 3:4). Confidence in God's promise to bring the believer into such a glorious revelation is based upon present hiding in Christ. Christian living has no splendor in the eyes of the world to whom a Christian is as good as lost. His life is buried in what they consider an unappealing cause; it is hidden with Christ in God. At Christ's coming the saved shall be revealed with Him, and He shall become Lord of lords and King of kings.

Paul, in writing to the Romans (8:17f.), said our suffering with Christ will be followed by a "glory which shall be revealed in us." In suffering together with Christ we enjoy the assurance of present sonship as well as the joy of anticipating the glorious manifestation at His coming. The Spirit's testimony agrees with our hope that we shall be glorified together with Him.

"If we are children of God, then are we His heirs, sharers of the heritage of Christ, i.e., partners not only of His sufferings but also of His glory. If so, they who, under the guidance of the Spirit, are crushing the appetites of their bodily life will share the eternal life of Christ: 'if by the Spirit ye are putting to death the actions of the body, ye will live.'"[8]

So Christ was once offered to bear the sins of many; and unto them that look for him shall he appear the second time without sin unto salvation—Hebrews 9:28.

Christ's first advent into the world was to "seek and to save that which was lost." As a sin offering He bore the sins of many "once for all." The work of redemption as it pertains to atonement for sin is entirely complete. When Jesus comes the second time, He will appear unto them that look for Him, but not to consider their sins. His first coming made possible the remission of sin and the power to overcome sin. His second coming is intended primarily to remove the church from the presence of sin. The Lord Himself shall return from glory in fulfillment of the announcement of His purpose and power to raise the dead in Christ first. "Then we which are alive and remain shall be caught up together with them in the clouds, to meet the Lord in the air" (I Thessalonians 4:17). This is the Christian's present and glorious hope of eternal salvation.

Our expectancy of the coming of our Redeemer is inspired by the hope of sharing His state of glory. We are now God's children, away from home, waiting for the manifestation of His Son. "We know that, when he shall appear, we shall be like him" (I John 3:2). Our full adoption, our coming into the full inheritance, is postponed until then. But the "we know" expresses the certitude with which we anticipate a share in the glorious event. We look for Him in confident waiting.

For the grace of God that bringeth salvation hath appeared to all men, teaching us that, denying ungodliness and worldly lusts, we should live soberly, righteously, and godly, in this present world; looking for that blessed hope, and the glorious appearing of the great God and our Saviour Jesus Christ; who gave himself for us, that he might redeem us from all iniquity, and purify unto himself a peculiar people, zealous of good works—Titus 2:11-14.

The Christian is constantly looking for the appearing of Christ with great anticipation of perfect happiness and absolute freedom. The grace of God which has brought salvation to all men teaches us that it is necessary to deny ungodliness and worldly lusts—that we should live soberly, righteously, and godly in this present life. The satisfaction of reality in Christian living and the testimony of the Spirit's presence in our lives gives hope of future eternal life.

There is no question as to what is meant by "that blessed hope." It is the glorious manifestation of our Saviour and the confident expectation of being present to participate in His glory. It is an intelligent assurance of the favor of God, centered in the coming of Christ.[9] It includes the resurrection from the dead, deliverance from the presence of sin, likeness to Christ, and the full realization of our sonship. It is an inward experience of filial confidence in God. In this respect faith in the future is the substantiation of things hoped for. "And we desire that every one of you do shew the same diligence to the full assurance of hope unto the end" (Hebrews 6:11).

"Cast not away therefore your confidence," referring to the confidence of hope, "for ye have need of patience" and of that hope wherein "faith is the substance of things hoped for." "And now, little children, abide in him; that, when he shall appear, we may have confidence," may not have lost it, and may "not be ashamed before him at his coming" (I John 2:28). Faith is certain now, as hope is conditionally certain, and must persevere, if it is not to be made ashamed. Here, then, is the confident expectation and bold expression of the full assurance of hope.[10]

[1] Watson, op. cit., p. 271.
[2] Beet, *Colossians*, p. 73.
[3] Torrey, op. cit., p. 484.
[4] Berkhof, op. cit., p. 58.
[5] Findlay, *Fellowship in the Life Eternal*, p. 53.
[6] James Denney, *The Second Epistle to the Corinthians* (The Expositor's Bible) (New York: Eaton and Mains, 1905), p. 54.
[7] Miller, *Ephesians*, p. 62.
[8] Beet, op. cit., p. 75.
[9] W. H. Griffith-Thomas, *St. Paul's Epistle to the Romans* (Grand Rapids: Eerdmans, 1946), p. 222.
[10] Pope, op. cit., p. 119.

7.

There Are Tests to Confirm Assurance

He that believeth on the Son of God hath the witness in himself: he that believeth not God hath made him a liar; because he believeth not the record that God gave of his Son. And this is the record, that God hath given to us eternal life, and this life is in his Son—I John 5:10, 11.

We turn now to the First Epistle of John. This is a letter that was written to Christian people to confirm their beliefs and to encourage Christian living. The primary purpose was to help readers who already believed that Jesus is the Christ the Son of God to reach the fullness of joy that comes from knowing the reality of eternal life. The repeated emphasis, occurring frequently throughout the entire epistle, is upon *knowledge.* It refers to the knowledge which one acquires through experience and which, therefore, brings certainty to the inquiring mind and confidence to the believing heart.

Sometimes the meaning of eternal life is stated as a great principle. At other times the idea is expressed as an exhortation to holy living. Occasionally it is expressed in terms of rejoicing in a great Christian privilege. A few times it is given in direct statement of a formal test. For the sake of uniformity and emphasis we have chosen to label all of them "tests."

The predominating idea in First John is to give the reader facts whereby he may know whether or not he has eternal life. Since "eternal life" is not the only term used to express salvation, we look for the same meaning in other forms. The many terms used by the writer also point out various phases of eternal life. He speaks of walking in the light, of having fellowship with God, of knowing God, of sonship to God, of dwelling in God, etc. All of these are single phases of salvation. We shall, therefore, proceed to discuss these tests in the form of checks by which the believer can confirm what he believes about his spiritual experience.

It seems a word of caution should be given at this point. The tendency to rely too fully upon conclusions drawn from comparisons of Christian graces with the requirements of God is dangerous. The self-examination involved in making such comparisons cannot be altogether reliable. The person who looks in his heart and judges it must remember that by nature he is inclined to minimize his own sinfulness and corruption. For that reason we need to take into consideration all the factors we are able to assemble and use the total picture rather than any one single test. This will serve to confirm the conviction already present.[1]

There is another caution to be offered. A person who gives himself a severe examination through conscious self-inspection usually finds in himself a great deal of failure. At first it may result in discouragement and fail to produce the glad assurance he anticipated. He is also in danger of reasoning in circles, when he searches for the proof of faith in his own works, which are the fruit of faith. For these reasons self-examination requires balance in thinking and honesty in application of the principles.

The Test of Character Involves Moral Purity

If we walk in the light, as he is in the light, we have fellowship one with another, and the blood of Jesus Christ his Son cleanseth us from all sin—I John 1:7.

"God is light." Christ came to reveal that Light by perfect demonstration of the will of God. Through our knowledge of God and of His will, we learn the secret of genuine happiness. The person who walks in the light is conformed to the will of God. It is not a test of profession, but a test of purpose and aims in life. Is your love motivated by the love of God? Is it a witness to the grace of God? Do you glorify God? If, in this self-examination, you find evidences of Christian character, that you are walking in the light and not in the darkness of sin, you have a proof of fellowship with the Father and of the cleansing effect of the blood of Jesus Christ.

This test rests upon the argument that God is the source of eternal life. In order to obtain that life, it is necessary to have fellowship with God. One who has fellowship with God must therefore be one who is walking in the light. This is not the light of feeling, but the light of fact.[2] By looking within his heart one can know whether or not he has turned away from darkness and is following the light he receives from the revelation of God. The emphasis is upon the word "walk." The ground of assurance is not merely knowing the light, but it is knowing that we walk in the light. It is possible for some people to surround themselves with human lights and see only the progress of human achievement. The light of God reveals the state of man in comparison with divine righteousness.

Another way in which one can ascertain this "walk in the light" is to examine his personal choices. The person who chooses constantly those areas of experience where there is fellowship with God is assured of salvation. It gives him a sense of friendship in divine society. He has a companionship in which conduct is influenced by the divine Presence.

People who walk in the light as God is in the light seek after moral purity. They are honest and strive to live by the truth. They keep God's precepts and are sensitive to the commandments of the Word. To them life is an open book which seeks to hide nothing. They do not hesitate to submit their lives to the most rigid investigation.[3] They are willing to have their deeds brought out into the light. When a person finds in himself such a willingness and openness with reference to his Christian walk and sees by such an investigation that it compares favorably with the will of God, he has passed the first test and has at least this one confirmation of eternal life.

The Test of Confession Involves Spiritual Cleansing

If we confess our sins, he is faithful and just to forgive us our sins, and to cleanse us from all unrighteousness—I John 1:9.

The person who "walks in the light" is living in great nearness to the Father. Being so close to the holiness of God makes one aware of his own unfitness for such royal fellowship. For that reason, a believing soul seeks constant cleansing. He dare not be deceived in this matter; he must frankly confess his need of repeated cleansing. He is like one who comes out of a coal mine into a brilliant light and sees the reflection of his blackened face. Looking about him and seeing well-groomed guests in the room, he feels unfit for the association of his friends. He seeks quickly for some method of cleansing before he appears formally in their society. So it is to come into the light of God. A believing soul does not deceive himself by saying that he has no sin. He confesses his need and finds forgiveness and cleansing through the blood of Christ. Fellowship with God brings a deepening sense of sin and so demands one confession after another. The process of cleansing therefore continues from day to day.

This verse has in it two elements of spiritual experience. The one is forgiveness which requires continued acknowledgment of personal sins. The other element is moral renewal, a continued cleansing from unrighteousness.

It is essential to understand the implication of the word "confess."

It is something more than mere assent to a statement of sin. The word used here has in it the idea of "saying the same thing that another says."[4] So the truly penitent and believing person will say the same thing about sin that God says about it. God has already spoken in His Word, so that we may know His attitude toward sin. Our inner voice must, therefore, say the same thing the Word says about sin. This is no time to soften the meaning of iniquity, and it is no place to condone what God condemns.

Note the significance of the plural word "sins." This is more than a general acknowledgment of belonging to a family of sinners. It is not referring to the depraved nature and its tendencies. It touches upon personal action and requires the confession of specific sins. Genuine confession of sins is associated with specific declarations of having done wrong.

The test is made very easily. We know we may claim the promise of God's forgiveness upon the condition of confession. When we confess our sins and our need of a Saviour, when we accept the divine plan for reconciliation with God, we are meeting the requirements of the Gospel. Having met these conditions, we have the assurance of eternal life.

The Test of Obedience Involves Divine Truth

And hereby we do know that we know him, if we keep his commandments. He that saith, I know him, and keepeth not his commandments, is a liar, and the truth is not in him. But whoso keepeth his word, in him verily is the love of God perfected: hereby know we that we are in him—I John 2:3-5.

The argument of this passage leads to the same definite conclusion as the preceding ones. We know that we are in Christ, that is to say, we know we have eternal life because we are keeping His commandments. The two tests which follow are directly related to this and grow out of the same general principle, love. The test of commandment-keeping deals with the broad principle. What we have labeled the tests of "love" and "loyalty" are specific applications to our relations with the brotherhood and to our relations with the world respectively.

To know that we have eternal life, that is, to know that we have fellowship with God, requires knowledge of vital experience. To know God in that sense implies an attitude of loving obedience. This test of Christian experience accordingly is stated in terms of commandment-keeping. It measures our experience by the fact of abiding in God and by a life patterned on the life of Jesus. Abiding in God yields the true knowledge of Him, a knowledge that is derived from experience with Him, and that is proved by obedience to command. To walk as Christ walked with God produces an awareness that we lovingly keep His Word. Such a walk becomes a token of reality in Christian experience.

This is a most reasonable measure of Christian experience. To profess to abide in Christ when not walking "as he walked" (verse 6) is a plain contradiction. Jesus taught this principle to His disciples, saying, "If ye love me, keep my commandments" (John 14:15). Any person who finds a disagreement between his profession and his practice can easily tell there is something wrong. If the profession of love for Christ is a mere feeling and does not induce obedience, we may well doubt the possession of eternal life.[5] Commandment-keeping is the objective test of fellowship with God, and love is its characteristic mood.

The contradiction of profession and practice provokes an uncompromising judgment, "the truth is not in him." When people profess to know God, but by their deeds deny Him (Titus 1:16), there is no other answer. Verses 8 and 9 in I John 1 indicate that the "Pharisaic moralist" who declines confession and claims he has not sinned is a liar. Here the indictment is pronounced against any "immoral religionist" who disregards the commandments of God. He, too, is a liar.

Genuine love for God, sincerity of Christian profession, and depth of spiritual experience all demand consistency in practice. One who presumes on God's mercy and who discounts the guilt of sin in deliberate transgression thereby shows he is ignorant of God, or else he has no will to keep His commands. There is more hope for a reckless, prodigal transgressor than for him.[6]

The word "keep" has special significance. As a military term it was used to describe the watch of a soldier who was keeping guard at his post. Its use here in a spiritual sense means "keeping our eyes on the commandments of God."[7] It requires an unbroken watch, a steady attention. Man is so prone to become preoccupied with worldly inducements that he forgets. The Christian must be on the alert always to recognize in every issue of life the expressed will of God.

"Keeping God's commandments" involves more than the mere doing of what is prescribed without a conformity of the will. "It signifies observant care, as of one keeping a safe path or a cherished trust." The Christian holds sacred any command of God for its own sake; he has respect for the One who has given it. Such respect mingled with genuine love makes obedience a principle. Loving God with mind, soul, and strength has a direct bearing upon moral action. It gives quality to obedience and leads to spiritual achievement.

Faithfulness to God's Word proves the extent of love. Where it is "kept"—apprehended, cherished, and held fast—there is evidence of eternal life. It is proof of fellowship with God.

The Test of Love Involves Social Compassion

He that saith he is in the light, and hateth his brother, is in darkness even until now. He that loveth his brother abideth in the light, and there is none occasion of stumbling in him—I John 2:9, 10.

We know that we have passed from death unto life, because we love the brethren. He that loveth not his brother abideth in death. Whosoever hateth his brother is a murderer: and ye know that no murderer hath eternal life abiding in him. Hereby perceive we the love of God, because he laid down his life for us: and we ought to lay down our lives for the brethren. But whoso hath this world's good, and seeth his brother have need, and shutteth up his bowels of compassion from him, how dwelleth the love of God in him? My little children, let us not love in word, neither in tongue; but in deed and in truth—I John 3:14-18.

In the test of obedience we were pointed to the underlying general principle that governs the Christian life. Love to God forms the motivation for obedience. This test, love for the brotherhood of saints, becomes a specific application of the general principle considered in the foregoing discussion. It puts assurance on the basis of evidence derived from ethical tests.

The principle of "love for the brotherhood" is essentially a trait of the new life. Unless our love for God is demonstrated in human relationships, the experience of spiritual life is inadequate. While love for God is a principle that controls the entire life, it finds a direct expression in desire for the fellowship of the saints.

The apostle says, "Whosoever hateth his brother is a murderer." This refers to one who refuses to be reconciled with his brother, or who holds a perpetual grudge. It describes the person who can see his neighbor in need without giving him help and is characteristic of one who can use selfishly the resources of another. Such traits of character are a manifest evidence of a lack of spiritual life.

Hatred toward a brother refers particularly to the state of mind and heart which harbors anger, malice, or envy, not to the incidental provocation that may arise in the Christian's life. If a person does not love habitually, that is, if selfishness and hatred are prevailing characteristics of his life, it is clear proof that he has not passed from death unto life.[8]

This love for our brethren, as a proof of regeneration, must go beyond mere feeling or human impulse. It consists of something more than deeds of helpfulness and devotion to our neighbors. It requires more than giving aid to one who is needy and more than sympathizing with a person who is sick. These are marks of human love for mankind. The test of assurance is made on the basis of the kind of love that finds its root in the love of God, that holds a favorable attitude toward brethren, because they are the children of God. That is, we love them on the strength of their being members of the family of God.

This love for the brotherhood is a distinguishing mark of Christians. It puts us into the class of Abel as contrasted with the class of Cain. It forms solid ground for the claim of eternal life. This is indicated by the fact that we act differently toward our brethren than we do toward people who are walking in darkness. It means that we hold the saints in high esteem and have a peculiar delight in brotherly relationships with them. Any person who habitually misunderstands and dislikes his fellow Christians evidently is not walking in the light. By the same token, when we habitually incline toward the wishes of our brethren and have a tendency to place the best construction upon their actions, imputing good motives to their deeds, we give evidence of eternal life.

There is, perhaps, no other line of evidence more personal or more specific than the test of brotherly love. It is a factor affecting the total pattern of Christian behavior. If brotherly love is lacking, all other evidences of eternal life are discounted.

The test of love is perhaps the clearest and most reliable combination of inner and outward evidence of eternal life. It furnishes decisive proof. This evidence of divine sonship, as expressed in our love toward the brethren, is very conclusive. To experience the controls of love in our social relationships, that is, to have a consciousness that love is ruling supremely is an indisputable evidence of the genuineness of spiritual experience. It is also equally true that the absence of this quality gives evidence of failure to have passed from death unto life. The Christian who can give a sincere testimony that he possesses a genuine love for his brethren has evidence within himself that he has passed from death unto life.

The Test of Loyalty Involves God's Will

Love not the world, neither the things that are in the world. If any man love the world, the love of the Father is not in him. For all that is in the world, the lust of the flesh, and the lust of the eyes, and the pride of life, is not of the Father, but is of the world. And the world passeth away, and the lust thereof: but he that doeth the will of God abideth for ever—I John 2:15-17.

This is another test directly related to the principle of love as discussed in the two foregoing divisions. We do not mean to imply that the apostle is attempting to give us a system of ethics. He is, rather, giving a series of tests by which the Christian can determine his spiritual standing. He is handling with precision a number of related points and is careful to make sure that he will not be misunderstood. He does not want to leave Christians in uncertainty about their spiritual condition.

We have considered the test of obedience as it involves our relationship to God and of love as it involves our relationship to our fellow Christians. In this discussion we face the test of love tried at the doorstep of the world.

This passage has in it another direct accusation which we dare not bypass. One who loves the world does not have the love of God in him. This means, therefore, that he does not have eternal life. A worldly heart is not subject to the rule of the Father and is therefore disowned in heaven. A person who courts the favor of the world, who follows its fashions, and who delights in its pleasures gives evidence that he loves the world.

The world about which we speak is the society of unbelieving people characterized by attitudes of indifference and godlessness. We refer to the sphere of spiritual darkness, the state of society as sin marred it. It is the channel through which Satan commits his crimes against the kingdom of God. Whatever puts God out of one's thoughts, whatever weakens the power of Christianity over the soul, whatever hinders one from doing God's will, whatever sets itself up to violate the love of God—be it unwillingness to forsake father or mother for Christ, or desire to indulge in sensual pleasure—this all belongs to what is understood by "the world."[9]

The world is in opposition to God. For this reason it is necessary to draw a line for the Christian, indicating what is permissible and what is forbidden with reference to human relationships. Anything that draws the affection of the heart away from God is definitely wrong. The contrast between the church and the world cannot be denied. The saints are characterized by love for the brethren, having a mutual affection which binds the Christian community together in a common persuasion and practice. Through this social and spiritual drawing together there is a definite withdrawal of Christians from the Christ-rejecting society about them. An intimate friendship between the people of the world and the children of God is a contradiction of Christian faith. The passions and pursuits of the worldly mind are altogether contrary to the delights and activities of the spiritual mind. Unbelievers do not affiliate with those who are genuinely devoted to Christ. Jesus said, "If ye were of the world, the world would love his own: but because ye are not of the world, but I have chosen you out of the world, therefore the world hateth you" (John 15:19). This division follows a genuine spiritual experience.

In this passage there are three categories of moral evil named as characteristics of the world's ungodliness. They are lust of the flesh, lust of the eyes, and pride of life. The lusts of the flesh include corrupted bodily desires. They are the perverted desires which tend to enslave the soul. A yielding to the cravings of physical desire, under circumstances that are morally forbidding, constitutes a lust of the flesh. The general characteristic of the world attitude is to disregard the moral implication and to indulge the flesh. This category of sin includes every form of license that goes beyond the boundaries of temperance and chastity. The lust for strong drink and indulgences in sexual vice are among the most conspicuous forms.

The second category of worldliness is described by the phrase, "the lust of the eyes." This refers to a different kind of temptation. The inducement to evil is made more particularly to the aesthetic sense, to the mind and to the imagination. When these desires are divorced from all thought of God and from obedience to Christ and are allowed to prevail over spiritual interests, they constitute lust of the eyes.[10] When things "to look upon" are allowed to gain supremacy over the things to be obeyed, the prevailing characteristic belongs to the world. In far too many cases aesthetic delights are displacing the nobler ideals and devotion to God. G. G. Findlay touches a vulnerable spot so delicately and describes so well that particular phase of worldliness that we quote him at length. "There is the world of dress and fashion, which exists for the eyes alone. What excitements, temptations, heart-burnings, follies, extravagances it contains! How large a part of human life—of the exercise of thought and skill, of the manifestation and the testing of character—revolves about the question, 'Wherewithal shall we be clothed?' The exercise of taste, the sense of fitness and beauty, in matters of personal appearance and social intercourse, of expression and handiwork, are inborn faculties. These sensibilities belong to our God-given nature; in the higher forms of genius, they bespeak an inspiration of the Almighty; but they have their diseases and excesses. The craving for adornment, and for the luxuries of beauty, grows by indulgence into a veritable *lust*, that may be as lawless and wasteful as any sensual appetite. There is nothing which makes a human being more frivolous and heartless, which eats away more completely the spiritual capacities, than the unbridled passion for dress and display."[11]

Observe also what Findlay has to say about the fine arts and their abuse. "The world of art has its idolatries, its revolts, its meretricious elements. St. James was a Hebrew puritan—the last man in the world to appreciate Hellenic art, but he has written the history of its fall: 'Lust, when it hath conceived, bringeth forth sin; and sin, when arrived at full growth, bringeth forth death' (James 1:15). God's curse fell in blight and defacement and shameful ruin on all that magnificent classic civilization. Restraint, reverence, is half the secret of noble craftsmanship. When it grows blind to the beauty of holiness, when it forgets its spiritual idea and gives the rein to licence, art loses its vigour in losing its purity; its loveliness allies itself to foulness, and becomes a horror. The motto, 'Art for art's sake,' if this signifies indifference to the religious interests of life and repudiation of ethical motives, is sheer idolatry; it means the enthronement of pleasure in the place of duty. Sterility is the doom of such isolation, in any field of human work. Impotence comes on every faculty that severs itself from the kingdom of God and withholds its tribute to His glory."[12]

The third category is called "the pride of life." This is more literally translated "the vainglory of life" and includes the pride of place, of position, and of possession. It indicates a disposition to "show off" at the expense of others. The rich man may become proud of his money or houses or lands. The vain woman becomes proud of her beauty and of the admiration of others, of her jewels and her fashionable dresses. The lawbreaker is proud of his exploits, intrigues, and clever escapes. The artist may become proud of his genius and works of art. A preacher may become proud of his large audiences or of his outward success. There is a sense in which persons of any position who compare themselves favorably with others to attract attention to self are indulging in a form of pride. All these are marks of worldliness; they are not of the Father.

This description of worldliness forms a basis upon which the Christian can examine himself. The believer who finds in himself a growing displeasure with the world and its follies, a widening gap between his interests and those of the world, and who finds world indulgences distasteful, has an evidence of his own attachment to the kingdom of God where purity and righteousness prevail. To be conscious of an increasing strength of the love of God in his own heart, as compared with love for the world, gives the Christian an awareness of good and righteousness in his own life.

[1] Berkhof, op. cit., p. 67.
[2] Keppel, op. cit., p. 20.
[3] James M. Ghysels, *The Highest Fellowship* (Grand Rapids: Zondervan Publishing House, 1936), p. 34.
[4] Ghysels, op. cit., p. 34.
[5] Keppel, op. cit., p. 37.
[6] Findlay, *Fellowship in the Life Eternal*, p. 136.
[7] Ghysels, op. cit., p. 55.
[8] Ghysels, op. cit., p. 160.
[9] Findlay, *Ephesians*, p. 199.
[10] Charles R. Erdman, *The General Epistles* (Philadelphia: Westminster Press, 1925), p. 124.
[11] Findlay, op. cit., p. 204.
[12] Ibid., p. 205.

8.

There Are More Tests to Confirm Assurance

The Test of Perseverance Involves Consistent Practice

Let that therefore abide in you, which ye have heard from the beginning. If that which ye have heard from the beginning shall remain in you, ye also shall continue in the Son, and in the Father. And this is the promise that he hath promised us, even eternal life— I John 2:24, 25.

Once more we strike the keynote of the epistle, but this is a test of a little different variety. John was writing in a time when evil influences were pressing in against the life of the church. These Christians to whom he was writing were facing a strong tempest of persecution and the subtle attack of heresy. In the verses preceding the passage quoted above, there is a brief description of the nature of the error to which he refers. The upshot of their heresy was the denial of Jesus as the Christ, the Son of God. There were many such antichrists whose influence was threatening the fellowship of the believers with the Father and the Son. It was a real threat to the believers' experience of eternal life.

In order to counteract these hostile influences among Christians, the writer calls attention to the foundation of their faith, insisting there is no reason for Christians to be moved away from the truth. In fact, he says he is writing to them because they know the truth, because they have "an unction from the holy one," and because they "know all things." This means that they had the witness of the Spirit within, that they had the testimony of the truth which they believed, and that they had the witness of the living Christ, all of which are pledges of eternal life. The note of confidence is an indication that the apostle does not expect men who have tasted these good things of the heavenly gift to be moved away from the old faith by false teachings.

In our own time the foundations of true faith are being tried severely. Old heresies, new theologies, unbalanced faiths, and compromising confessions are gaining popular favor. Pragmatic and naturalistic philosophies have made serious inroads into Christian thinking. The standards of morality have been "watered down." The conscience has been seared, and the church is condoning practices which are in direct violation of the Word of God.

The "many voices" in the world keep clamoring for attention. The moralist makes constant vigorous effort to build good character. He regards the failure of man a weakness to be corrected by moral disciplines; he does not call it sin. He believes human nature is essentially good and simply needs improvement. In the process of self-cultivation, he congratulates himself and commends his own virtues. He denies any need of Christ as a Saviour.

There are many self-made people in the world who style themselves educationists. They hold that if people had more opportunity to know they would be less immoral. They seek to build a better society by improving the environment, believing that better conditions will produce better life. Theirs is a form of social gospel which denies the need of supernatural experience. They miss the point entirely of regeneration and the transforming work of the Holy Spirit.

Another class of active promoters of good are called philanthropists. They look for salvation, not so much in the building of character nor in the accumulation of knowledge and culture, but in gaining the favor of God through service, by the things they do. They claim that good works will not be rejected. They insist that efforts to relieve sorrow and oppression, that giving to the poor, and that contributions of money to great causes serve in a mediary function to please God. They deny the need of Christ's intercession and of His atonement.

There are many religionists who hope to gain salvation through outward observances. These we call the ritualists. They hope that by their observance of the various forms of worship they will gain the favor of God. They seem to think there is saving power in the sermons delivered at the church and in the ordinances observed there. Actually, however, personal experience with God through the Lord Jesus Christ does not depend upon ritual. The observance of ritual provides a channel of divine blessing, but is not the source of it.

Another form of Christ-denial is expressed in the philosophy of the rationalist. He insists that everything he believes must correspond with the conclusions of reason. He does not hesitate to reject anything in the Bible which does not conform to his processes of reason. It is essentially a religion that eliminates the supernatural. Therefore he denies that Jesus was born of the Virgin Mary, and denies that Jesus was the Christ.

It is in the face of such influences that we need to apply the test of perseverance again in our day. It is not enough to have begun well. The promise of eternal life is given to the person who firmly holds the truth concerning the deity and death of Christ and concerning the resurrection and exaltation of the living Lord. So long as we hold this Word and its related truth, Christ has promised to abide in us forever.[1] A Christian profession that is characterized by stability of faith and consistency of practice gives evidence of genuineness. Experience of the joy of assurance rests also upon continuance in the things which we have been taught by the Lord. To withdraw from our dependence upon Christ or to deny the truth about Him is to forfeit fellowship with the Father. The promise of eternal life is to those who abide in the Gospel.

The Test of Conduct Involves Doing Righteousness

And now, little children, abide in him; that, when he shall appear, we may have confidence, and not be ashamed before him at his coming. If ye know that he is righteous, ye know that every one that doeth righteousness is born of him—I John 2:28, 29.

Whosoever is born of God doth not commit sin; for his seed remaineth in him: and he cannot sin, because he is born of God. In this the children of God are manifest, and the children of the devil: whosoever doeth not righteousness is not of God, neither he that loveth not his brother—I John 3:9, 10.

We have described the filial life of the believer as sustained by various aspects of experience. We have seen the evidence of reality in one who "walks in the light," who confesses his sins, who keeps the commandments of God, who "loves his brother," who "loves not the world," and who lets the truth abide in him. Now this test gives evidence that "one who does [executes] righteousness" possesses eternal life. He is one who proves himself a son, born of God. This therefore takes us into the realm of "the practice of righteousness."

There are three reasons mentioned in these passages which can be united to give a sense of certainty to the child of God: the indwelling of the Spirit, the believer's confidence at Christ's coming, and the new birth. Since we have dwelt at length upon the evidence one receives from the presence of the Holy Spirit, we shall not go into that here. It is important at this point, however, to know that the presence of the Spirit in the life of the believer is a reason for being able to live the righteous life. He is operating from within giving proper motivation and power of will to choose the right. It is the presence of the Holy Spirit in the believer which makes possible holy living. Therefore one who lives a holy life has the evidence of the Spirit within; he has eternal life.

The hope of Christ's return and its relation to assurance has been discussed in a previous division. We notice here that the anticipation of His coming increases the Christian's desire to avoid being ashamed when He appears; it has a definite influence upon the Christian's conduct. This is also related to the evidence it brings of the reality of Christian experience. One who hopes to see God face to face will strive earnestly to keep himself pure for that occasion.

The third reason, the fact of our having been born of God, comes as a new aspect of assurance. We shall dwell at greater length upon this point to show how the fact of having been born of God is evidenced by the life we live. Daniel Kauffman says, "The Bible is not wanting in evidences whereby we may know whether or not we are the children of God."[2] He discusses "the most prominent" among them, namely, (1) righteousness, (2) sinless life, (3) Spirit-led life, (4) obedience, (5) love, (6) hatred of evil, (7) faith, and (8) the victorious life. He says, "The children of God, as far as they have the light, love the things which God loves and hate the things which He hates. . . . Everyone that is an ardent lover of that which is good is also a strong hater of that which is evil. This is one of the fundamental evidences of sonship."

There is no righteousness apart from a right relationship with God through the Lord Jesus Christ. Righteousness in the believer is a sign of sonship. This is practically the same principle Jesus taught when He said, "By their fruits ye shall know them." It is a test which we frequently use in our human relationships. Even the world itself insists upon "the product." So in an objective examination of the religious experience of others, as well as in an introspective examination of ourselves, the same test applies in judging the genuineness of Christian profession. It stands to reason that the real child of God will do what is right and will keep from evil.[3]

The righteousness referred to in these passages expresses the thought of the habitual quality of the Christian's life. Light begets light; the nature of God is imparted to His children. The righteous Father has righteous children, but not the kind which are good only occasionally. Righteous living is to the child of God as regular as is breathing. It happens sometimes that a person walking along the sidewalk stumbles. He does not stumble every step that he takes. If he did, some neighbor would likely come to his assistance and escort him to the doctor's office. Stumbling is the occasional occurrence; walking upright is the habitual experience. For many weeks he may go up and down the streets without stumbling, and yet it is possible that he may one day be embarrassed with the experience. So it is in the life of the Christian. He may fall into sin, but it is not his habit. He regularly conforms to the will of God and lives in accord with His standards of life.

We have seen that the promise of eternal life is to those who abide in Christ. This test points up additional evidence to prove that we are abiding in Him. We know that we are begotten of Him by the doing of righteousness. When we subject ourselves to an earnest examination on the point of conduct and sit in fair judgment upon ourselves, we find that the disposition to do the will of God evidences our having been begotten of Him.

In the second passage quoted above there is a direct statement indicating that one who is born of God does not commit sin. The construction of this in the original language emphasizes the idea of practicing sin. It means that one who is born of God does not continue in the practice of sin. His habitual manner of life is righteous; he does not continue on in sin. In verse 29 of the second chapter, the appeal is made on the basis of personal knowledge of ordinary fact. "Ye know" indicates a simple perception in which one concludes normally that such will be the case.

There is nothing in these passages which teaches the believer to think that his good works will improve his salvation; rather, they present the form of evidence by which one can assure himself that he has eternal life. It is as much as saying that the quality of conduct which he discovers in his own life could not have been achieved by himself, but that it is the product of divine grace. The doing of righteousness, that is, conforming to the will of God, is a sure sign of having been born again.

The negative approach to this test has a bearing also on the matter of assurance. Since we recognize that sin is lawlessness, then the person who habitually commits sin has not only gone aside from the will of God but he has actually been doing what the law of God forbids. The person who does this must know therefore, that he is not begotten of God. The divine grace that came to him at the new birth and which constituted him a child of God is made void. How can he continue to be a child of the holy God while he ignores, or even defies, the law of God?[4] If a person is acting lawlessly, doing what he knows to be sinful, no profession can make him a child of God.

"The proof of being a Christian is found in the life one lives." This test of conduct is a most simple application of the great principle of righteousness. One who knows that he is conducting himself rightly, who knows that he is conformed to the will of God, has the evidence of genuine Christian experience. Because he walks in righteousness he shall not be ashamed at His second coming.

The Test of Conscience Involves Approved Behavior

And hereby we know that we are of the truth, and shall assure our hearts before him. For if our heart condemn us, God is greater than our heart, and knoweth all things. Beloved, if our heart condemn us not, then have we confidence toward God. And whatsoever we ask, we receive of him, because we keep his commandments, and do those things that are pleasing in his sight— I John 3:19-22.

The conscience is an instinctive power that enables a person to distinguish between right and wrong—a gift which God gives to man through the natural processes of generation. It serves inward notice to the person either accusing or approving individual behavior. It is the moral power in man that enables him to discover his own standing with God and with men.

The normal attitude of the child of God is to have confidence toward his Father. Just as children feel free to go to their parents with their needs and wants, so the child of God does not hesitate to approach the Father, telling Him all his troubles, seeking advice, stating problems, and confessing sins. A Christian who is properly taught and who understands his filial relationship with the Father has this confidence. In case he should be attacked by accusing thoughts, he is able by an appeal to his conscience to convince himself of his assurance, because he knows the approval of God. This enables him to approach God with humble confidence as an accepted son.

In the verses preceding the passage quoted above the emphasis lies in the direction of sincere love of the brethren and all people of the community. (Read verses 14-16.) This, as we saw in an earlier discussion, is a sign of the presence of divine love in the heart (page 71). Having applied the various tests to which we have been introduced, we have yet to reckon with the fact of the inner judge that resides in the soul of man. There is no use to set up against the conscience any mere sentiment without facts. This passage says, "God is greater than our heart." To be sure, God is willing to forgive those things upon which our heart dwells in penitence. This removes the occasions for the accusations of the conscience. One must always guard against any attempt to set up a vain assurance. There is no natural way in which the heart can be reconciled to sin without doing damage to the conscience. Any superficial settling of the conscience by overpersuading the heart to believe a thing contrary to fact is not clearing the conscience. Where there is real ground for self-condemnation there must be an appropriation of divine grace for forgiveness. With a consciousness of forgiven sin, the heart can then again rest assured of fellowship.

The foregoing tests are not intended to override the dictates of a sensitive conscience. The Holy Spirit, who forms a very satisfactory ground of evidence, brings no contrary evidence against the voice of man. "God the Holy Ghost does not in His testimony supersede conscience: He honours that ancient representative of the Divine voice within the nature of man; and never disjoins His evidence from that of the subjective moral consciousness which condemns or approves—in this case approves—according to the standard of law written on the heart, or the conscience—'and knoweth all things.' He knoweth the mystery of the Atonement and may silence the condemning heart. But if He assures of pardon He commits the assurance to the conscience as its guardian."[5]

After the warning against a false peace (verse 20), comes the reassuring refrain of verse 19, "Hereby we know that we are of the truth," our hearts are assured before Him, for we have "confidence toward God" (verse 21). This confidence reflects the experience of peace, of joy, of freedom, of love, and of righteousness in the happy child of God. It indicates that the child is speaking to the Father with a trustful heart.

There are reasons, however, for persons to withdraw from the presence of God. When the heart lacks confidence, there is something wrong. The person who is afraid to go to Him must have some hindrance in the way. Sometimes a person who is asked to speak to another is hesitant to make the approach. He is afraid for some reason and does not want to go. He lacks the necessary freedom or inclination to go. There may be two possible reasons for this. The person to be approached may have an unfriendly attitude. Or the trouble may lie within the person who is to take the initiative. He may have done an injury to the other party and for that reason his conscience troubles him. So it is in our approach to God. We know that He is never unfriendly to the voice of penitence and to the cry of need. If there is any hesitance to approach God, the fault must lie within the person who should approach Him. If his conscience is troubling him, then the wrongdoing must lie close home.

The greatest hindrance to confidence is sin. People are afraid to approach God because of transgressions; guilt lies in the way. The conscience speaks and makes the person afraid to approach God. This may apply to wrong relationships with our fellowmen or wrong attitudes toward God. God is ready to forgive, however, whenever the self-accusation is justified. On the other hand, God is not to be deceived by an overconfidence any more than by a self-accusing attitude. People who disregard their inner misgivings must face the fact of judgment.

It is definitely stated that this matter of assurance has a direct relationship to our prayers. When the heart is condemned on any score, there is fear of God. When there is no condemnation, there is hope in God. The abiding favor which gives answers to our prayers rests upon the principle of righteousness. Here appears another form of the test of righteousness. We get answers to our prayers because we live pleasingly before the Father. It also reflects the principle of commandment-keeping. The loyal heart is quick to court the pleasure of God and will therefore receive answers to his prayers. In this way, the answer to prayer becomes a token of our acceptance with God and an assurance of His pleasure.

The tense of the verb "condemn" is significant. It is put in the tense of the Greek present, indicating continuity. A continuing condemnation of the heart is an unwholesome condition of life. The repeated or sustained protest of conscience must be satisfied. This is not referring to any mere misgivings of a sensitive nature, nor does it refer to any disturbance caused by minor irregularities. The condemnation of God rests upon those who allow irregularities to become a habitual practice or a settled condition. If there is no such persistent condemnation, we are confident of a favorable relationship with God; we have assurance of salvation.

The Test of Experience Involves Spirit Witness

And he that keepeth his commandments dwelleth in him, and he in him. And hereby we know that he abideth in us, by the Spirit which he hath given us—I John 3:24.

Hereby know we that we dwell in him, and he in us, because he hath given us of his Spirit—I John 4:13.

In this test we move away from the faculty of the conscience to experience with the Holy Spirit. In addition to the evidences we have found in other areas, we have the witness of the Spirit from the fact of His indwelling presence. Whereas the test of conscience is applied to the inward states and conditions of life, this added witness comes from without. This has to do with the knowledge of what Christ has done for us through the power of the Spirit. It is a consciousness of possessing eternal life, the sort of thing of which we cannot be conscious unless it is an actuality.

The teaching of John Wesley lays great stress upon the testimony of the Spirit and insists that it cannot be separated from fruits in the life of the believer. This means that He always concurs with the facts of the life in which He lives. The presence of love, joy, peace, long-suffering, gentleness, goodness, faith, meekness, and temperance is in keeping with a pronouncement of the Spirit.[6] In addition to the display of moral virtues, the Christian hears the divine voice within his soul and knows by that experience that he is a child of God. In one sense the presence of virtue is in itself a witness of the Spirit. When the believer has divine love in the heart, when he has a consciousness of filial relationship with God, when he experiences a sense of reverence and obedience to God, when he realizes that there is in him a voice of intercession, when in time of suffering he experiences comfort from the Spirit, when he becomes aware of strength in time of need, and when he has victory in seasons of temptation—all being works of the Holy Spirit—he knows he has eternal life. Insofar as we discover these virtues abounding in us, they bear the witness of the Spirit to the reality of our Christian experience.

Another principle of experience with the Spirit is the concurrence of His witness with the facts revealed through other tests. The Person who has inspired the Word will always give a testimony that agrees with the description of an assured state. The inward cleansing of the soul and the outward victory in conduct are the work of the Spirit. When a person is fully aware of cleansing and victory, he knows the Spirit is in agreement with the evidence produced by any specific test such as the test of loyalty. So in every other test, as that of character, confession, obedience, love, perseverance, conduct, and conscience, the Spirit always agrees.

At this point we must express a note of caution. There are many false "isms" in the world making claims of eternal life similar to that of Christianity. We may be sure that not all which claims to be of God is actual Christian experience. People are deceived by false teachers, by antichrists. This means that, while the witness of the Spirit is most precious when it is genuine, it is also very apt to be counterfeited.[7] Therefore we must be extremely cautious in accepting claims to the witness of the Spirit, whether it is in our own experience or in the profession of others (cf. 4:1). In line with the discussion on the test of perseverance, we wish to call attention again to the evidences of genuineness in Christian profession. The Spirit of God will always confess that Jesus Christ is the incarnate Son of God. The Holy Spirit will always lead into controversy with the world and give victory over it. The Spirit is loyal to the teachings of Christ. He does not speak in contradiction to any part of the revelation of God. By these simple tests one can know the strange voice of a false teacher.

In the list of evidences supporting genuineness of Christian experience we have included the experience of love. The Spirit of God does not prompt hate, but He Himself is of the essence of love.

The presence of the Holy Spirit cannot be manifested through any other temperament than that of love. Since love has its source in God, its presence in our lives indicates that we have fellowship with Him. Knowing that fellowship with God is eternal life and having warm feelings of goodwill toward men, we conclude that we have the Holy Spirit.

The Holy Spirit becomes a voice of divine assurance. Just as a person is convinced of the reality of those things which he has seen with his own eyes, so one is convinced with the reality of eternal life through the experience of the heart. To know that the power of God has touched his life gives the believer a consciousness of the Spirit's presence. This is not a self-generated confidence, nor is it acquired by any process of reflection. It rests upon the facts which follow in the experience of one who believes in Jesus Christ.[8] The "well of water springing up" in the heart of the Christian, as promised by Christ Himself, lies deeper than human nature. This is, as Jesus said, the gift of God, the Holy Spirit. We know that God dwells in us by the fact that we have the Holy Spirit; and the Spirit is witnessing to us by His presence. A man who is physically alive knows it from the consciousness of life itself. In the same way spiritual life is the evidence of the presence of the Holy Spirit. The fact and witness must agree.

In the realm of experience we can test the reality of our Christian life by what the Holy Spirit does and is. To know that He leads us is proof that God has given Him to us. To know that the Spirit has been given to us is an evidence that God abides in us. This witness of His Spirit with our spirit becomes a blessed assurance of eternal life.

And we know that the Son of God is come, and hath given us an understanding, that we may know him that is true, and we are in him that is true, even in his Son Jesus Christ. This is the true God, and eternal life—I John 5:20.

The Test of Belief Involves Faith in Christ

And this is his commandment, that we should believe on the name of his Son Jesus Christ—I John 3:23a.

Every spirit that confesseth that Jesus Christ is come in the flesh is of God—I John 4:2.

Whosoever shall confess that Jesus is the Son of God, God dwelleth in him, and he in God—I John 4:15.

Whosoever believeth that Jesus is the Christ is born of God—I John 5:1a.

These four references to an active faith in Christ express a major factor in the foundation of spiritual kinship. The first (3:23) sets up the condition of believing in the truth of the revelation as it pertains to Christ. The second and third are forms of recognition of Christ as being both human (4:2) and divine (4:15). The fourth (5:1) presents faith in its most personal and direct form. Here in this last passage we view faith in its full and definite sense of appropriation. True faith takes hold of truth and gives expression to it in human behavior. It not only admits the truth about Christ's incarnation but enters into direct relation with Him as Lord of all of life.

The crucial test of Christian belief lies in the confession that Jesus is the Christ. What a Christian confesses, whether by lip or by life, is essentially what he believes. A confession of Jesus Christ involves what one does about His claims to deity and to humanity. To have eternal life requires faith in the incarnation of Jesus. To believe that He "is come in the flesh" declares two things: first, that He was a pre-existent One who is "come" from heaven; second, that He was truly man, having come in the "flesh." This is the only kind of person, a God-man, who could actually become our Saviour.

The love of God is expressed most perfectly in the giving of His Son to die for the ungodly (Romans 5:8). Any theory that makes Christ less than divine robs the Gospel message of its unique testimony to God's love. If Christ was not divine, John 3:16 is meaningless. Faith in the Sonship of Christ is the channel through which the love of God is made intelligible to the world.[9]

Believers are assured of the truth of the Gospel by believing in Jesus Christ. We learn that He is the only One who could in any way take away our sins and relieve the guilty conscience. He has made it possible for us to draw near to God "in full assurance of faith." That is to say, faith in such a Person brings into our experience the powers of a new life—the communications of life by the eternal Spirit—and we have both a satisfactory condition of heart and an acceptable approach to God.

"He that believeth on the Son hath everlasting life" (John 3:36a). God has spoken through His Son and has confirmed it by the experience of the apostles. This gift of eternal life may be received consciously by all who believe. If this statement cannot be accepted at face value, then there is no remedy for anxiety, fear, tormenting anticipation, or doubt. If our believing is in vain, there is no freedom of soul, no happiness, no rejoicing. Let us believe and have joy! Let us trust God entirely and receive all He bestows. If we have faith in Christ, we have God's written testimony that we have eternal life, that our sins are forgiven, that we are His dwelling place, that we are His children, and that we are heirs of His eternal inheritance.

[1] Findlay, *Ephesians*, p. 225.
[2] Daniel Kauffman, *Doctrines of the Bible* (Scottdale, Pa.: Mennonite Publishing House, 1928), p. 295.
[3] Keppel, op. cit., p. 55.
[4] Ibid., p. 59.
[5] Pope, op. cit., p. 121.
[6] Cannon, op. cit., 219.
[7] Keppel, op. cit., p. 73.
[8] Findlay, op. cit., p. 296.
[9] Ibid., p. 346.

9.

We Heed Warnings to the Christian

There are passages of Scripture which admit the possibility of lapse from grace. The problem of harmonizing these with those that give assurance of eternal life is not at all difficult if we recognize the conditions of salvation. (See chapter 1.) In this chapter we shall examine Scriptures which declare the possibility of losing our standing with God. The next chapter points to the abundant provision of divine grace that makes possible complete victory. We will see in chapter 10 that the individual believer must accept God's plan and method of salvation and that he is directly responsible, as a free moral agent, to maintain proper attitudes, to exercise a "faith which worketh by love," and to cultivate the graces which sustain spiritual life.

Wherefore the rather, brethren, give diligence to make your calling and election sure: for if ye do these things, ye shall never fall —II Peter 1:10.

In the verses preceding this passage, Peter outlined a course of Christian growth. The divine nature imparted to the believing soul needs exercise to produce fruit. "Progress in Christian living is made only by co-operation of the human will with the divine."[1] To make the "calling" and "election" sure requires a holding fast to the Gospel. The Apostle Peter admits that "it is within man's power to frustrate both and that effort was required to give them permanent validity."[2] The calling of the Gospel and the election to the fellowship of the saints are parts of God's covenant but it remains with the believer "to ratify or rescind" the conditions of receiving divine grace. These virtues have no "purchasing power" in relation to securing divine favor. They are rather the means of sustaining kingdom benefits, of making "sure" the fulfillment of God's purpose in the calling and election. Diligence (i.e., "labor with most intense purpose of soul") in exercising such faith is a guarantee against falling.

It is the possibility of falling away that inspired so many warnings in the Scriptures against carelessness, against sinful indulgences, and against all kinds of behavior that deserve the displeasure of God. These warnings are given with the hope that Christians will refrain from sinful indulgences and escape the consequences of evil. They are given to alert the believer in these perilous times so that he may be kept from falling.

Avail Yourself of Divine Grace

We then, as workers together with him, beseech you also that ye receive not the grace of God in vain—II Corinthians 6:1.

The context of this passage refers to the wonderful provision God has made through giving His own Son as a sin offering for us. This He did that we might be made the righteousness of God in Him. For that reason the Apostle Paul urges his readers to avail themselves of the privileges of the Gospel in order that they receive not the grace of God in vain. As he stated in his First Epistle to the Corinthians, it was from him they had received the Gospel wherein they stood. Now he was concerned that they should testify of the things which they had known of Him. If they should refuse or neglect to be witnesses, "workers together with him," they would have received God's favor to no purpose.

There is another application of this appeal. Those who are reconciled through Christ should walk according to the new life in Him. To walk according to the flesh is to receive the grace of God "for an empty thing." Failure "to put to practical use in the details of life the spiritual benefits received by the favor of God, even His favor, becomes to us a useless thing."[3] The implication goes deeper; it involves both state and standing with God. Whedon includes in his commentary the significant rendering of Erasmus, "That ye may not so transgress as that, having once been exempted from your sins, ye may be relapsing into your former life, have received the grace of God in vain."[4]

Commit Yourself to Divine Truth

Ye therefore, beloved, seeing ye know these things before, beware lest ye also, being led away with the error of the wicked, fall from your own stedfastness—II Peter 3:17.

In his letters to the dispersed Christians Peter wrote to help them in their relationships to hostile people under adverse world conditions. In the second epistle he wanted to stir up their minds by way of remembrance that they should not forget the commandments which the apostles of the Lord had given them. He was very conscious of those who would lead them astray. Near the close of his second epistle he gives the striking admonition quoted above, which recognizes by divine inspiration the possibility of their being led away by the error of the wicked. He warns them to be diligent lest they fall from their own steadfastness.

To fall from steadfastness is to allow the arguments of false teachers to move you away from the truth of the Gospel. Christians are warned here to be careful and watchful—to guard themselves against the dangers from without. The wicked, the lawless, have their way of wresting the meaning of Scriptures so as to make themselves feel safe to sin. To join that company of false leaders would lead to shipwreck of the whole Christian life.[5]

The word translated "fall" is the same as that used in Acts 27:29 translated "fallen" as referring to shipwreck. The sailors feared being cast ashore among the rocks. The warning in Peter is against moral peril, the error of the wicked. This is the same as aimless wandering, sailing without a rudder, living without a plan, or living in doubt and uncertainty. The steadfastness from which people fall refers to firmness of belief, strength of conviction, and purposeful activity. The warning is an admission: error leads men away from God.

Protect Yourself With Divine Righteousness

Now the Spirit speaketh expressly, that in the latter times some shall depart from the faith, giving heed to seducing spirits, and doctrines of devils—I Timothy 4:1.

This epistle contains strong admonitions to a young minister who was bearing the responsibility of one who must give account for the souls of men. Paul refers to God's prediction that people will depart from the faith. In doing so they will give heed to seducing spirits and doctrines of demons. From this we may well conclude that men can be and will be alienated from God. Timothy was instructed to put the brethren in remembrance of the faith and of the good doctrine which he himself had received. He was charged with the responsibility of organizing churches so as to protect the interests of truth. He was to place into positions of leadership men who were given to right living and sound teaching.

Apostasy refers to a falling away from the truth and righteousness. It expresses itself in various shades of unbelief and in many forms of corrupt practices. It is brought about by the influence of false teachers who cause Christians to lose faith and to sear the conscience. The major emphasis of this passage is to guard against allowing such hostile forces to have access to members of the church lest they might be led astray. It leaves no doubt as to the possibility of being led away from God. It is stronger than that; it declares the fact that some will depart from the faith. The assumption is unmistakable; it is possible to be led astray. Be very careful therefore to maintain good doctrine and purity of life.

Identify Yourself With Divine Revelation

For I testify unto every man that heareth the words of the prophecy of this book, If any man shall add unto these things, God shall add unto him the plagues that are written in this book: And if any man shall take away from the words of the book of this prophecy, God shall take away his part out of the book of life, and out of the holy city, and from the things which are written in this book—Revelation 22:18, 19.

This passage follows the wonderful invitation which the Spirit and the bride announce when they say, "Come." "Whosoever will" is invited to take of the water of life freely. But in consideration of all the many promises of honor, praise, and blessing to the children of God, the writer of the Apocalypse wishes to emphasize the importance of full acceptance of the message of his prophecy. The promise has been given to those who "do his commandments, that they may have right to the tree of life, and may enter in through the gates into the city." To tamper with this prophetic message, to wrest the meaning of the Scripture from its divine purpose, is such a serious offense that God will act in judgment upon any who are guilty of mishandling this Scripture.

Tampering with the Word involves more than additions and subtractions from the text. It includes corruptions of the truth and detractions from the message. It applies also to attempts to destroy the effect of the message and to efforts that seek to undermine its authority.

While the warning pertains directly to this Book of the Bible, it must be remembered that the Apocalypse is rich with New Testament truth. To challenge the doctrines of the Revelation is to challenge the Gospel; one who questions the Gospel is questioning his own salvation.[6]

It seems very significant that within each of the three parts of the Old Testament Scripture, the Law, the Psalms, and the Prophets, there is a caution against improper attitudes toward the Word of God (cf. Deuteronomy 12:32; Proverbs 30:5, 6; Malachi 4:4). Here at the close of the New Testament canon we meet it again. It emphasizes a vital aspect of personal obligation and of the Christian attitude. Here the warning indicates the possibility of losing part in eternal blessedness.

Subject Yourself to Divine Discipline

I therefore so run, not as uncertainly; so fight I, not as one that beateth the air: but I keep under my body, and bring it into subjection: lest that by any means, when I have preached to others, I myself should be a castaway—I Corinthians 9:26, 27.

The great apostle, who on so many occasions gave expression to his filial confidence in God, to the certainty of his position in Christ, to the evidence of the Holy Spirit's leading, and to the possession of Christian character, now says that he keeps under his body, bringing it into subjection lest by living after the flesh (Romans 8:13) he should become one rejected. This is not to be understood as referring to qualification for the conflict but "to be unsuccessful in the issue." He realized that unless he brought his body, his physical appetites and passions, under the control of reason and conscience he was in danger of losing out in the race.

Although eternal life is received as a gift from God it is sustained by contest and victory.[7] The body must be subdued for holy purposes. It dare not curtail devotions on account of weariness, it dare not shrink from duty because of unpleasantness, and it dare not indulge in pleasure at the expense of kingdom interests. It must be kept under to reach the goal of eternal happiness.

A sound belief in Christian assurance must be accompanied by the conviction of the possibility of failure and of the necessity of using our utmost to reach the final goal.[8] The experiences of divine favor in the past are no guarantee of unconditional favor in the future. There is danger of being a castaway through neglect or transgression. The first ten verses of the tenth chapter of First Corinthians use the story of Israel to prove that those who stand may fall. The judgment inflicted upon them because of their repeated offenses against God is used as an evidence that God does not hold Himself bound to save one who deliberately disobeys. This disobedience includes indulgence in evil desires (lust), adopting substitutes for God (idolatry), conforming to world standards (fornication), accepting borderline practices (tempting Christ), and jealousy over the fortunes of others (murmurings). Repeated offenses of this kind under the Christian economy merit the same judgment. There is no time for complacency in the Christian conflict.

Condition Yourself to Divine Purposes

Now the just shall live by faith: but if any man draw back, my soul shall have no pleasure in him—Hebrews 10:38.

The writer of Hebrews in the context which precedes this verse, stated that we have need of patience (endurance), that, after having done the will of God, we might receive the promise. Then he refers to the imminent coming of Christ. In this passage he emphasizes the nature of our relationship with God. Ours is a life of faith; "the just shall live by faith." In the following statement, according to the Greek construction, he refers to that "just one" who lives by faith as being the one who might draw back. A more literal rendering therefore would read, "But if a just man draw back, God shall have no pleasure in him." The insertion of "any man" so as to avoid the implication that a "just man" may fall away is altogether unwarranted.[9] The context following states that "we are not of them who draw back unto perdition; but of them that believe to the saving of the soul." This passage recognizes the possibility of a just man's drawing back from the faith. "Take heed, brethren, lest there be in any of you an evil heart of unbelief, in departing from the living God" (Hebrews 3:12).

Throughout this epistle there is nothing to substantiate the dogma of "final perseverance."[10] There are at least five insertions in the main argument which constitute warnings against the perils of apostasy. The first is an appeal for diligence lest we drift (2:1-4). The second is an urge to steadfastness to avoid departing from God (3:7-14). The third calls for growth to maturity in spiritual experience to avoid spiritual degeneration (5:11-14). The fourth is this appeal for endurance to avert the danger of apostasy (10:36-39). Last of all is the need for active service to escape the judgment of God (12:25-29).

It is not essential that we dwell any longer on this side of the issue. We have submitted enough Scriptural evidence to prove the possibility of falling from grace. Nor does this argue that it is at all likely that a true believer will draw back into perdition. It must be the exception rather than the rule. The warnings are intended to help honest souls avoid the perils of apostasy, and we believe faithful preaching and teaching of the Word is a good antidote to evil influences. In proportion to his belief and practice of the Scriptures, the Christian has the effect of that blessed assurance of salvation which so completely satisfies the true child of God.

---

[1] Erdman, op. cit., p. 92.

[2] J. J. Lias, *The First Epistle to the Corinthians* (The Cambridge Bible) (Cambridge: University Press, 1892), p. 169.

[3] Joseph A. Beet, *Epistles to the Corinthians* (London: Hodder and Stoughton, 1885), p. 384.

[4] D. D. Whedon, *N. T. Commentary* (New York: Hunt and Eaton, 1875), Vol. IV, p. 169.

[5] J. Rawson Lumby, *The Epistles of St. Peter* (The Expositor's Bible, New York: Eaton and Mains), p. 373.

[6] D. D. Whedon, *N. T. Commentary* (New York: Hunt and Eaton, 1880), Vol. V, p. 483.

[7] Beet, op. cit., p. 159.

[8] Christian Friedrich Kling, *The First Epistle of Paul to the Corinthians* (Lange's Commentary) (New York: Scribner and Co., 1868), p. 201.

[9] Brooke F. Westcott, *The Epistle to the Hebrews* (London: Macmillian and Co., 1889), p. 337.

[10] F. W. Farrar, *The Epistle of Paul the Apostle to the Hebrews* (The Cambridge Bible) (Cambridge: University Press, 1893), p. 160.

10.

God Makes Provision for Victory

For whatsoever is born of God overcometh the world: and this is the victory that overcometh the world, even our faith—I John 5:4.

There is no need for Christians to be unhappy or to live in moral defeat. There is no need to fear being unable to reach heaven. Such reflections can be ruled out of the Christian's life easily and simply. Failure in Christian experience is due to failure to appropriate the grace of God. There is abundant provision for constant victory over sin.

He Keeps Us from Falling

Now unto him that is able to keep you from falling, and to present you faultless before the presence of his glory with exceeding joy —Jude 24.

In this familiar but precious benediction, Jude commits his readers to the One who is able to guard them from stumbling. In the context preceding he dwelt upon the various ways in which men stumbled and fell. He gave some severe and somber warnings against such great wickedness as was found in those who had turned away from God. He reminded them of God's terrible judgments against the evil found among those who professed to know Him. Now, in the conclusion of his short epistle, against a background of justice, he paints the bright picture of divine love. God is both ready and able to protect those who cling to Him.

There are two assumptions implied in this verse: that there is danger of falling, and that the Christian purposes are to be kept. There are many obstacles in the way, there are dark scenes of perplexity, there is much suffering, and there are some who have gone into apostasy. Christians need protection in the midst of such hostile influences lest they fall. But God has made provision for His children to be guarded against any pitfalls or snares of the devil. He has provided means by which Christians can be kept in the presence of moral perils and present sorrows. A garrison of divine power, the merits of our Redeemer, the virtue of His intercessions, and the indwelling of the Holy Spirit are all set up in triumphant opposition to the forces of apostasy. We may all expect victory.

The second assumption refers to verses 20 and 21. God is able to keep those who build themselves up in a progressive faith, who pray in the Holy Spirit, who keep themselves in the love of God, and who look with expectancy for the mercy of our Lord Jesus Christ. Those who meet these conditions qualify for the service of His guarding agents; any such are assured that God will keep them.

"He that dwelleth in the secret place of the most High shall abide under the shadow of the Almighty" (Psalm 91:1). There is absolutely no question about God's ability, nor is there any doubt concerning His willingness to keep us from falling. As the leaves of a tree protect us from the sun's ray as long as we keep ourselves in its shade, so the power of God keeps us from falling as long as we abide in Him through trustful and obedient living. The will of man is free to act according to individual choice; if he determines to abide in "the secret place" he will be safe.[1]

He Keeps Deposits Available

For the which cause I also suffer these things: nevertheless I am not ashamed: for I know whom I have believed, and am persuaded that he is able to keep that which I have committed unto him against that day—II Timothy 1:12.

There is tremendous responsibility in being appointed a preacher of the Gospel. As an apostle and teacher of the Gentiles, Paul no doubt recalled such perilous circumstances as those which he encountered in Jerusalem when the Jews accused him of polluting the Temple by bringing into it a Gentile convert. But, in spite of it all, he was neither ashamed nor afraid. He had committed himself to God who had called him to be an apostle to the Gentiles, who ordained him to preach the Gospel to them, and who led him to give his testimony before hostile Jews. He was convinced that this same God is able to keep that which he had committed unto Him. In the light of these facts, he enjoined upon Timothy to "hold fast the form of sound words" and to "keep," by the aid of the Holy Spirit, that good thing which was committed unto him. He was assured that after so doing he could depend upon God's keeping power.

That which Paul committed to God was a "deposit" to be guarded unto the day of Christ's coming. Whether that deposit referred to his reward, his soul, his salvation, his faith, his apostolic office, or all of these, makes little difference to the purpose of this discussion.

The writer is inclined to the view that Paul refers to his own spirit, soul, and body. He is ready also to make application of the principle to anything personal in which a believer acts, anything that lies within the power of man's choice to entrust to God or to withdraw from His care. The persuasion is the same, that whatever is placed within the range of God's protection will lie safe in His hands.[2] We are confident of His abiding and effectual care.

Such assurance belongs to every Christian. He can rejoice in the Gospel under all circumstances. He finds personal satisfaction in Christian service even though it involves great sacrifice and much difficulty. He lives in constant triumph over fear and anxiety. He lives "in the light of deathless hope."

He Guards His Own

Who are kept by the power of God through faith unto salvation ready to be revealed in the last time—I Peter 1:5.

An incorruptible inheritance is reserved for the redeemed. In the meantime we pass through manifold temptations which may severely try our faith. This should cause no alarm, for God has very graciously provided protection for the hour of temptation. "There hath no temptation taken you but such as is common to man: but God is faithful, who will not suffer you to be tempted above that ye are able; but will with the temptation also make a way to escape, that ye may be able to bear it" (I Corinthians 10:13). We have an High Priest who can be touched with the feeling of our infirmities. He "was in all points tempted like as we are, yet without sin. Let us therefore come boldly unto the throne of grace, that we may obtain mercy, and find grace to help in time of need" (Hebrews 4:15, 16).

Peter, as quoted above, uses the Greek word translated "kept" which carries the sense of "guarded"—"Who are guarded by the power of God." This indicates a hedge of protection similar to that which God set up around Job. Although Job was a man of indisputable integrity, Satan sought to dissuade him from his trust in God. The devil was limited in his power. So God limits the power of Satan now when he seeks to overthrow the Christian through various forms of temptation. Besides, our Father has provided a sympathetic High Priest upon whom we may rely for effectual mediation in our times of need.

The use of the present participle gives an interesting shade of meaning. It indicates that the "guarding" is "something in progress, a continuous process of protection."[3] In the preceding verse reference is made to the inheritance reserved ("laid up and kept") for you. This is a perfect participle, "which has been reserved," indicating that the inheritance has been and is under guard in heaven. It is kept absolutely secure in heaven for those who are being guarded on earth. It is being protected in a garrison, by the power of God in view of the Christian's faith in Him.

We need not fear the enemies of salvation. We are surrounded by a protecting "bodyguard." We are in a favorable position, in a strongly garrisoned fortress. It is an assured position secured by the same means through which we obtain salvation, through faith. If we hold our confidence steadfast unto the end, our hope will become a reality of eternal possession "revealed in the last time."

He Saves Completely

Wherefore he is able also to save them to the uttermost that come unto God by him, seeing he ever liveth to make intercession for them—Hebrews 7:25.

This verse declares the perfection of salvation. Christ has entered into the presence of God for us. He is there to plead our case before the Father. "We have an advocate with the Father, Jesus Christ the righteous" (I John 2:1). There is absolutely no fault with God if a soul is lost. "For he that cometh to God must believe that he is, and that he is a rewarder of them that diligently seek him" (Hebrews 11:6).

The person who comes to God in simple but sincere faith has the assurance that God is able to save completely. The Lord has provided a means of victory for everyone who will earnestly appropriate the merits of His intercession. God is able to save completely and to give victory, because Christ is interceding for you.

Christ is able to save because He has made satisfactory atonement for sin and because He continues to make intercession perpetually. He has taken care of the sins of the past and is now engaged in taking care of the sins of the present. "The power of His heavenly life implies the highest development of moral condition."[4] He has entered the holiest place to stand in the presence of God for us continuously.

The salvation secured by the living Intercessor is complete, reaching every element of man's nature and spiritual need.[5] The function of the perfect High Priest is to take an active share in working out salvation in those who have received the Gospel. At every moment of trial the divine aid is available. Provision has been made for complete victory over sin.

His Love Is Inviolable

For I am persuaded, that neither death, nor life, nor angels, nor principalities, nor powers, nor things present, nor things to come, nor height, nor depth, nor any other creature, shall be able to separate us from the love of God, which is in Christ Jesus our Lord—Romans 8:38, 39.

The context of this passage refers to tribulations, distresses, persecutions, famines, poverty, perils, and the sword. The apostle was confident that in all these things the child of God is more than a conqueror through Christ who loved him. He has a strong persuasion that none of these afflictions shall move him from his confidence in God, nor from his position in Christ Jesus our Lord. He believes firmly that no such experience will keep God from loving the victim of hostile circumstances. It was a settled principle with him that the powers of men, and even the providential occurrences which might come into his experiences, should not interfere with his relation to God. The Christian has this confidence that God will protect His own, even though he may be subjected to severe testings in trials and afflictions.

The love of God is essential to His nature. He would not be God if it were not for His love. His affection for the believer is far more than a passing surge of temporary emotion. It is a steadfast devotion to the welfare of all who trust in Him. When distress, perils, or persecutions fall upon the believer, there is no withdrawal of His love. His divine nature is unchangeable and is not modified by earthly conditions. We can always rely upon a sympathy, a caring that is motivated by true love.

The entire last half of this eighth chapter of Romans follows the theme of suffering unto glory. The plan of God, the work of Christ, and the intercessions of the Spirit are all combined to meet the great need of human redemption. Human powers cannot overthrow the plan, man cannot annul the work of Christ, nor can the enemies of God interfere with the pleadings of the Spirit. The inheritance is secured, the provisions are adequate, and the means are all available. God's love is a sure refuge for the sinner and is an inviolable right to the Christian.

He Approved the Son

But ye believe not, because ye are not of my sheep, as I said unto you. My sheep hear my voice, and I know them, and they follow me: And I give unto them eternal life; and they shall never perish, neither shall any man pluck them out of my hand. My Father, which gave them me, is greater than all; and no man is able to pluck them out of my Father's hand. I and my Father are one—I John 10:26-30.

On a previous occasion the Pharisees had understood that Jesus claimed equality with God. At this time when our Lord spoke these words quoted by John, the same issue was up again. The words are the reply Jesus gave in response to their request. "If thou be the Christ, tell us plainly." He had told them before but they would not believe Him. The printed verses are the explanation why they did not understand. Had the Jews believed that Jesus was the Messiah, the Son of God, they would have been counted among the sheep who knew His voice.

This passage declares the essential unity of the Father and the Son. What one does is backed by the other. What one promises will be fulfilled by the other. There is no disagreement between them. A sheep under the Shepherd's care, one who follows Jesus, is most surely God's own. There is no way of alienating a sheep from either, without at the same time wrenching him from the hand of the other. "I and my Father are one." The relationship of man with either or both must be considered in the light of this unity.

Here is the promise of eternal life. It is supported by the authority of God and by the integrity of Jesus Christ. It implies the tenderest shepherd care of the Son with an equal emphasis upon the care of the Father. Such divine unity, supporting the purposes of redemption, inspires absolute confidence in the claims of Christ. Our faith in Him invokes the blessing of the eternal Father.

From the viewpoint of human responsibility we must recognize three conditions: Eternal life is given to those who "hear" His voice, who "know" Him, and who "follow" Him. "Hearing his voice" is a condition of obedience which keeps us in a position where God can keep us and protect us from the enemy. "Knowing" emphasizes the factors of fellowship. "Following Him" emphasizes the need of keeping in the will of God. If we do these things we shall never fall. What if a sheep refuses to hear any longer? What if a sheep refuses to follow? What if a "just man" draws back? God has no pleasure in him.

The reverse is equally as convincing. If we have heard His voice in acceptance of the Gospel, if we know His voice in terms of fellowship, and if we are following Him in terms of service, we have the assurance of acceptance with the Father. God has made provision for our needs in His Son.

He Qualified Our Advocate

For Christ is not entered into the holy places made with hands, which are the figures of the true; but into heaven itself, now to appear in the presence of God for us—Hebrews 9:24.

The function of our High Priest is to offer daily intercessions for us. Christ is engaged in a perpetual cause. We have in Him an Advocate to plead every case that needs reconciliation with God. He is in "heaven itself" appearing now "in the presence of God for us" so that "if any man sin" there is an open channel to the throne of judgment for a righteous settlement of the case.

This is a great provision for the life and soul of the believer. It is an adequate means of dealing with the problem of sin in the Christian's life. It is the secret of victorious living. The believer who becomes aware of sin in his life looks immediately for mercy and asks for forgiveness. The blood of Christ is the only remission of sin and the only basis of approach to God. That is why the crucified but risen and exalted Son is accepted (legally qualified) to plead the case in the royal court. He bears the marks of supreme sacrifice, securing thereby pardon for the penitent soul and power to overcome his next temptation.

In First John the apostle's reference to the believer's sins and to the righteous Avocate admits the possibility of lapse from grace.[6] He asserts that relief from any such case is afforded at once by the intercession of Christ. This is not to be taken as a license to sin; that would be taking base advantage of a gracious privilege. Any presumption that regards it safe to sin because of this provision puts the believer into a perilous position, indeed. To think that one can stumble along and never utterly fall, to expect that willful transgression will be forgiven automatically, or to indulge in forbidden pleasure, thinking that the Mediator will take care of each sin in successive order—these attitudes are far from the intention of God. The arrangement is set up for the accommodation of the occasional incident in spiritual tragedy. This is truth applied in an "emergency ward."

In the Scripture passages quoted in this section, reference is made to divine provision for victory in human experience. They point to the keeping power of God and to the conditions upon which the believer appropriates His sustaining grace. The promises of God are as sure as His own existence. We have no occasion to feel the least uncertainty about our present standing with Him nor of our prospects of final triumph. It is only self-confidence and self-effort that runs aground. Full trust in God, complete confidence in Christ, and constant yielding to the Spirit lifts upward to the Light.

[1] Alfred Plummer, *The General Epistles of St. James and St. Jude* (The Expositor's Bible) (New York: Eaton and Mains, 1905), p. 465.
[2] Henry Alford, *The New Testament for English Readers* (Cambridge: Deighton, Bell, and Co., 1866), Vol. II, Part II, p. 558.
[3] Marvin R. Vincent, *Word Studies in the New Testament* (Grand Rapids: Eerdmans, 1946), Vol. I, p. 631.
[4] Thomas C. Edwards, *The Epistle to the Hebrews* (The Expositor's Bible) (New York: Eaton and Mains, 1905), p. 129.
[5] Westcott, op. cit., p. 191.
[6] Findlay, *Ephesians*, p. 135.

11.

The Believer Is Responsible for Action

Grow in grace, and in the knowledge of our Lord and Saviour Jesus Christ—II Peter 3:18a.

The discussion which follows in this chapter is not to be understood to imply that sinful man can by any self-effort merit favor from God. What we have said before on this point and what follows here does not refer to any meritorious works. Man is wholly dependent upon divine grace for a Redeemer; there was no man of mere human generation that could qualify. In God the believer finds his source of power to overcome sin and the world. In himself he is too weak for the conflict. Christian living is a life of faith and trust.

Our mention of conditions of salvation and conditions of assurance refers to human response. God has spoken, God has offered His grace, God has promised, and God has sought out a people for His name. If there were no favorable human response, there would be no saving of souls. The benefits of grace, the possession of promise, and the satisfactions of divine fellowship can be realized only upon established conditions. These requirements are not of human device; they are stated in God's own revelation of Himself and of His plan to redeem. It is our purpose in this chapter to examine some of these conditions in order to discover the believer's responsibility toward sustaining eternal life and toward maintaining his assurance of salvation.

Keep in Memory the Gospel

Moreover, brethren, I declare unto you the gospel which I preached unto you, which also ye have received, and wherein ye stand; by which also ye are saved, if ye keep in memory what I preached unto you, unless ye have believed in vain—I Corinthians 15:1, 2.

The Gospel which Paul preached is based primarily upon two cardinal doctrines, the crucifixion and the resurrection of Christ. It was these and related truths that Paul had preached to the

Corinthians; it was these which they had received. It was the ground of their faith wherein they were standing; it was the means by which they were being saved. The present tense indicates a state of safety from the power and punishment of sin.[1]

The condition upon which the Christian experiences day-by-day deliverance from sin and from its consequences is "holding fast." This is a warning that suggests self-examination, forming an appeal to the reader to ground his faith in the real Gospel. It implies that victory comes in proportion to the firmness with which the believer holds fast to the teachings of the Word.[2] Salvation is secured by a firm maintenance of the accepted truth. Holding fast means more than intellectual keeping of the Gospel in memory; it refers to the practical regard for the truth in life and conduct. It signifies perseverance of faith.[3] It means the kind of believing that appropriates continuously the benefits of the Gospel.

The Christian is individually responsible for keeping a vital contact with the truth wherein he stands. He must prove his faithfulness in the grace he has received. The continuance of holding to the Gospel is proof of the continuance of the state of salvation.

Continue in the Faith

Yet now hath he reconciled [you] in the body of his flesh through death, to present you holy and unblameable and unreproveable in his sight: If ye continue in the faith grounded and settled, and be not moved away from the hope of the gospel, which ye have heard, and which was preached to every creature which is under heaven— Colossians 1:21-23a.

The apostle has declared the nature, office, and work of Christ. He brings his argument to a suitable climax when he makes the personal application to those who believe in Him. "You . . . hath he reconciled"—to present you to God in true holiness, that is, if you continue in the faith. The final benefits of our reconciliation with God, which was so graciously effected in Christ, are made conditional upon our continuance in faith. "A turning from the Gospel to some substitute would work a forfeiture of its promised results." The faithful child of God has this assurance, however, that a persistent and consistent life of faith is certain to be rewarded with a most glorious and final presentation to God.

The paraphrase of Lightfoot throws additional light on the meaning of this passage. "But now in Christ's body, in Christ's flesh which died on the cross for your atonement, ye are reconciled to Him again. He will present you a living sacrifice, an acceptable offering unto Himself, free from blemish and care and even from censure, that ye may stand the piercing glance of Him whose scrutiny no defence can escape. But this can only be, if ye remain true to your old allegiance, if ye hold fast (as I trust ye are holding fast) by the teaching of Epaphras, if the edifice of your faith is built on solid foundations and not reared carelessly on the sands, if ye suffer not yourselves to be shifted or shaken but rest firmly on the hope which ye have found in the Gospel."[4] This refers to a holding fast in simple reliance on the all-sufficient Saviour, precluding any substitute and insisting upon faithful adherence to faith in Jesus Christ.

John Wesley was a strong advocate of steadfastness. He insisted that faith can be lost through disobedience and a willful inclination to sin.[5] Then it follows that assurance fades out, and communion with God is cut off. In order to avoid losing out with God, the believer must exercise a living and continuing faith. One who is grounded in the knowledge and love of God, one who is firm and perseveringly settled in his loyalty to Christ, has assurance of the present state of salvation and has hope to enjoy heaven.

The condition stated in this passage is not inconsistent with assurance of salvation. It is a condition which encourages watchfulness and awakens a sense of personal responsibility. At no time is it used to cause misgivings. It merely emphasizes the necessity of having a present and continuous faith to remain in the benefits of divine grace. "Tomorrow must get its own grace by its own faith."

The "if" in this and other passages means that however great the powers of Christ are, however fixed the purposes of God may be, and however deep the desires of the Holy Spirit to secure the believer, there is no fulfillment of these without habitual exercise of faith.[6] The renewing powers of the Gospel are effective in those who keep in constant contact with Christ and who continue in fellowship with Him.

Abide in Christ

If a man abide not in me, he is cast forth as a branch, and is withered; and men gather them, and cast them into the fire, and they are burned. If ye abide in me, and my words abide in you, ye shall ask what ye will, and it shall be done unto you—John 15:6, 7.

We are wholly dependent upon the true Vine to sustain life. The fulfillment of the divine purpose is realized in the life of Christ and in the personal attachment of the believer to Him. What God intended originally in the creation of man is found in the incarnate Son.

Jesus used the illustration of the vine and the branches as a fitting symbol of our union with Him. The vine can bear no fruit if it has no branches. The branches cannot live without the vine. Together they constitute a fruit-bearing tree. If a branch does not bear fruit, it is cut off and cast away. The allegory cannot be mistaken. Christ needs the branches to bear fruit for Him and there is no fruit in the believer's life apart from a vital union with Christ.

"If a man abide not" and "if ye abide in me" are the phrases which determine the emphasis of this passage. The first presents the negative force of judgment upon an unhealthy condition of soul. Jesus refers to the point in time of the execution of the last judgment. He who will have fallen away from Him will be gathered with others of similar apostasy and cast into the fire.[7] This is a case in which one failed to abide in Him. The consequence that falls upon the nonabiding one is clear. The life he had while abiding in Christ has withered; it has perished and is appointed to the fire for "everlasting burnings."

The positive declaration is equally as emphatic as the negative. Here the figure ceases; the language becomes direct and loses its symbol. "If ye abide in me" postulates a necessary consequence. Such a person lives and prays in the name of Jesus. He receives answers to his petitions. That means his life is a glory to God, it abounds in love, it grows in obedience, and it finds fullness of joy.

Abiding in Christ refers to a spiritual condition which produces fruit. It implies loyalty to Christ both in faith and conduct. If the soul and Christ are really in vital union, there will be fruit; the life will serve a good purpose in the kingdom of God. Abiding in Christ guarantees continual personal communion with God. "If a man abide not in me, he is cast forth." "If ye keep my commandments, ye shall abide in my love." The responsibility of the believer cannot be mistaken.

Continue in the Word

Then said Jesus to those Jews which believed on him, If ye continue in my word, then are ye my disciples indeed; and ye shall know the truth, and the truth shall make you free—John 8:31, 32.

These words from the lips of our Master came immediately following an enthusiastic acceptance of His teachings among the Jews. Because so many professed faith in Him, He warned against a superficial discipleship. Jesus plainly states the condition upon which they may be assured of the permanent effects of the Gospel. If you continue in the Word, you shall learn to understand the truth. (John 7:17). Obedience to the Word is the way to find true liberty in Christ. You are the friends of Christ if you do what He commands (John 15:14). For He is "author of eternal salvation unto all them that obey him" (Hebrews 5:9).

To get a saving knowledge of divine truth and to be released from the bondage of sin requires reality in Christian experience. Jesus demands more than emotional attraction and passing belief; the requirement for discipleship is a settled commitment to the Word. This involves decisive action.

The meaning of the word *continue* enforces the requirement of deliberate and prevailing conviction. It refers to the necessity of making this a permanent condition of life.[8] It means more than merely "continue to believe"; it covers the entire scope of meaning in the word *abide*. It involves a perseverance that reckons with divine reality and that expresses itself in willing obedience to the Word.

True discipleship is an evidence of eternal life. The person who becomes a learner, in the true sense of divine enrollment, has continuous experience with the truth. Such experiential knowledge guarantees freedom, producing a genuine sense of belonging to Christ—"then are ye my disciples indeed."

The Christian is responsible individually to maintain a life that corresponds with the divine pattern. Experience and Scripture must coincide. The promises of the Word have force only on the basis of conformity to the standards of Scripture. If the Christian lives by the Word, he not only proves assurance of salvation, but he sustains his freedom in the truth.

Mortify the Deeds of the Body

If ye live after the flesh, ye shall die: but if ye through the Spirit do mortify the deeds of the body, ye shall live—Romans 8:13.

This passage contains a unique promise of life. Mortifying the deeds of the body is not a means of obtaining life but a means of maintaining it. The flesh represents the tendency with us to go wrong; in it resides inherited depravity. That person who wants to retain his spiritual relationship with God must recognize these inborn inclinations to do evil. He cannot hope for a complete wiping out of carnal desires; so he must be diligent in mortifying them. Fleshly appetites, if they are indulgently satisfied, lead away from God. The person who makes it a practice to live after the flesh will surely suffer spiritual death (separation from God).

The emphasis is laid upon the positive aspect of this condition: "if . . . ye shall live." Making use of the power of the Spirit in dealing with the flesh is a necessity in sustaining eternal life. The element of sinfulness in human experience calls for intense resistance of evil. The verb *mortify* in the present tense indicates a continued process of "making dead" the deeds of the body.[9] It is not a matter of eradicating the flesh but rather a continual slaying of the deeds that proceed from it.

Dealing with the deeds of the body requires more than human effort. It calls for the kind of discipline that surpasses reformation of acts and habits. This "doing to death the practices of the body" is accomplished by the Holy Spirit. "Through the Spirit" the believer counteracts the practices which the body would like to carry out. Improper lusts are conquered by yielding to the promptings of the Spirit and by using His power to overcome them. The Spirit is able to reduce such desires to nothing, delivering the trusting soul from the power and the consequences of evil deeds.

The responsibility of the believer lies in his making habitual use of the Spirit. God acts when man shows an inclination to have it so. The Spirit must be given control of the life before He can control the deeds. The believer, therefore, must yield to the Spirit with a disposition to cease from fleshly indulgence. He must be in a habitual frame of mind to have this desire slain and to enlist his will as an ally to the Spirit in the campaign against deeds and demons that displease God.

Hold the Beginning of Your Confidence

Take heed, brethren, lest there be in any of you an evil heart of unbelief, in departing from the living God. But exhort one another daily, while it is called To day; lest any of you be hardened through the deceitfulness of sin. For we are made partakers of Christ, if we hold the beginning of our confidence stedfast unto the end— Hebrews 3:12-14.

The preceding verses refer to the experience of Israel in their forty years of wandering in the wilderness. God was grieved with them (verse 10), because they were "a people of wanderers in heart." Their disobedience invoked the wrath of God with an oath that determined they should not enter into His rest. The promised inheritance of Canaan was lost to them. In fact, the pronouncement included more than one generation; the judgment fell heavily upon succeeding generations. The idea is carried over in this passage and applies to the rest that still remains for the people of God.[10]

The "take heed, brethren," forms a solemn warning to all believers. In the light of what happened to Israel, Christians must be careful lest the same tragedy fall upon them. This mention of Israel's failure to attain God's rest is followed by a direct application of their sad example to Christian experience. All Israel was baptized in the sea but the most of the Israelites failed to reach Canaan because of unbelief and disobedience. The warning is against apostasy such as characterized Israel.

The remedy is offered in verses 13 and 14. Exhortation from the brotherhood and steadfastness in the individual will keep from apostasy. Christians need to exhort each other daily. They need Christian fellowship for repeated mutual encouragement and inspiration. Unless there is earnest attention and mutual exhortation within the Christian group, there is danger of becoming hardened through the deceitfulness of sin.

Another appeal based upon the phrase "taking heed" is the caution to hold firmly our confidence in God. Continued trust assures continued fellowship with Him. It is not enough to commence the Christian life; we must hold the good beginning until Jesus comes. The promise of eternal blessedness rests upon continued faithfulness. The believer's responsibility to sustain this confidence in God continues unto the end.

[1] Lias, op. cit., p. 141.

[2] Beet, *Corinthians*, op. cit., p. 265.

[3] Kling, op. cit., p. 359.

[4] J. B. Lightfoot, *St. Paul's Epistles to the Colossians and to Philemon* (London: Macmillan and Co., 1876), p. 160.

[5] Cannon, op. cit., p. 68.

[6] Alexander Maclaren, *The Epistles of St. Paul to the Colossians and Philemon* (The Expositor's Bible) (New York: Eaton and Mains, 1905), p. 106.

[7] Heinrich A. W. Meyer, *Critical and Exegetical Hand-Book to the Gospel of John* (New York: Funk and Wagnalls, 1884), p. 431.

[8] Plummer, op. cit., p. 187.

[9] H. C. G. Moule, *The Epistle of Paul the Apostle to the Romans* (Cambridge Bible) (Cambridge: University Press, 1892), p. 146.

[10] Alford, op. cit., Vol. IV, p. 635.

Bibliography

Alford, Henry, *The New Testament for English Readers*. Cambridge: Deighton, Bell, and Co., 1866.

Austin-Sparks, T., *God's Spiritual House*. London: Witness and Testimony Publishers.

Beet, Joseph A. *Commentary on Colossians*. London: Hodder and Stoughton, 1890.
Commentary on St. Paul's Epistles to the Corinthians. London: Hodder and Stoughton, 1885.
The New Life in Christ. New York: Hunt and Eaton, 1895.

Berkhof, L. *The Assurance of Faith*. Grand Rapids: Wm. B. Eerdmans Publishing Co., 1939.

Cannon, William R. *The Theology of John Wesley*. New York: Abingdon-Cokesbury Press, 1946.

Dale, R. W. *The Epistle to the Ephesians*. New York: George H. Doran Co.

Denney, James. *The Second Epistle to the Corinthians* (The Expositor's Bible). New York: Eaton and Mains, 1905.

Edwards, Thomas. *The Epistle to the Hebrews* (The Expositor's Bible). New York: Eaton and Mains, 1905.

Erdman, Charles R. *The General Epistles*. Philadelphia: The Westminster Press, 1925.

Farrar, F. W. *The Epistle of Paul the Apostle to the Hebrews* (The Cambridge Bible). Cambridge: University Press, 1893.

Findlay, G. G. (ed.) *The Epistle to the Ephesians* (The Expositor's Bible). New York: Eaton amd Mains, 1905.
Fellowship in the Life Eternal. London: Hodder and Stoughton, 1849.

Ghysels, James M. *The Highest Fellowship*. Grand Rapids: Zondervan Publishing House, 1936.

Griffith-Thomas, W. H. *St. Paul's Epistle to the Romans*. Grand Rapids: Eerdmans, 1946.

Hastings, James. *The Christian Doctrine of Faith*. New York: Scribner's, 1919.

Kauffman, Daniel. *Bible Doctrines*. Scottdale, Pa.: Mennonite Publishing House, 1928.

Keppel, David. *That Ye May Know*. New York: Eaton and Mains, 1909.

Kling, Christian. *The First Epistle of Paul to the Corinthians* (Lange's Commentary). New York: Scribner and Co., 1868.

Lias, J. J. *The First Epistle to the Corinthians* (The Cambridge Bible). Cambridge: University Press, 1892.

Lightfoot, J. B. *St. Paul's Epistles to the Colossians and to Philemon.* London: Macmillan and Co., 1876.

Lumby, Rawson. *Epistles of St. Peter* (The Expositor's Bible). New York: Eaton and Mains, 1905.

Maclaren, Alexander. *The Epistles of St. Paul to the Colossians and Philemon.* (The Expositor's Bible). New York: Eaton and Mains, 1905.

Meyer, Heinrich, A. W. *Critical and Exegetical Hand-Book to the Gospel of John.* New York: Funk and Wagnalls, 1884.

Miller, H. S. *The Book of Ephesians.* Harrisburg, Pa.: The Evangelical Press, 1931.
The Christian Worker's Manual. New York: George H. Doran Co., 1922.

Moule, H. C. G. *The Epistle of Paul the Apostle to the Romans* (The Cambridge Bible). Cambridge: University Press, 1892.

Plummer, Alfred. *The General Epistles of St. James and St. Jude* (The Expositor's Bible). New York: Eaton and Mains, 1905.

Pope, William Burt. *A Compendium of Christian Theology,* Vol. III. Cleveland: Thomas and Mattill.

Simons, Menno. *Complete Works,* Elkhart, Ind.; John F. Funk and Brother, 1871.

Thorold, Anthony W. *The Presence of Christ.* Philadelphia: George W. Jacobs and Co.

Torrey, R. A. *What the Bible Teaches.* New York: Fleming H. Revell Co., 1898.

Smith, Hannah Whitall. *The Open Secret.* New York: Fleming H. Revell Co., 1885.

Vincent, Marvin R. *Word Studies in the New Testament,* Vol. I. Grand Rapids: Eerdmans, 1946.

Watson, Richard. *Theological Institutes.* New York: Phillips and Hunt.

Westcott, Brooke F. *The Epistle to the Hebrews.* London: Macmillan and Co., 1889.

Whedon, D. D. *New Testament Commentary.* New York: Hunt and Eaton, 1875.

Zeoli, Anthony. *Blessed Assurance.* Wyncote, Pa.: Evangelist Anthony Zeoli, 1942.